GCSE History is always topical with CGP...

Revising "Weimar and Nazi Germany, 1918-39" for Edexcel GCSE History is tough, but with this CGP Topic Guide you'll be all set for exam success.

It's packed with crystal-clear revision notes explaining the whole topic, plus plenty of helpful activities, sample answers, exam tips, exam-style questions and more.

How to access your free Online Edition

This book includes a free Online Edition to read on your PC, Mac or tablet.
To access it, just go to **cgpbooks.co.uk/extras** and enter this code...

1943 8893 7298 6700

By the way, this code only works for one person. If somebody else has used this book before you, they might have already claimed the Online Edition.

CGP — still the best! ☺

Our sole aim here at CGP is to produce the highest quality books —
carefully written, immaculately presented and dangerously close to being funny.

Then we work our socks off to get them out to you
— at the cheapest possible prices.

Published by CGP

Editors: Robbie Driscoll, Catherine Heygate, Katya Parkes, Jack Tooth.

Contributor: Paddy Gannon.

Reviewers: Ben Armstrong, Kate Black, Amanda Roper.

With thanks to Izzy Bowen and Charley Maidment for the proofreading.
With thanks to Jan Greenway and Emily Smith for the copyright research.

Acknowledgements:

Cover Image: Germany: Runners at the Brandenburg Gate at the start of the 1936 Summer Olympic Games, Berlin, 1936 / Pictures from History / Bridgeman Images.

With thanks to Mary Evans for permission to use the images on pages 4, 6, 10, 38, 40, 42, 44 and 50.

Extract used on page 9 reprinted by permission of Abner Stein and Don Congdon Associates, Inc. © 1960, renewed 1988 by William L. Shirer.

With thanks to Alamy for permission to use the images on pages 11, 29, 41, 51 and 62.

Extract used on page 13 from Access to History: Democracy and Dictatorship in Germany 1919-63 by Geoff Layton. © Geoff Layton 2009. Reproduced by permission of Hodder Education.

With thanks to Dr Ruth Henig for permission to reproduce the extract on page 17 from The Weimar Republic, 1919-1933 by Dr Ruth Henig in the Lancaster Pamphlet series.

Extract used on page 17 from A Brief History of The Third Reich: The Rise and Fall of the Nazis by Martyn Whittock, published by Little, Brown Book Group.

Image used on page 20: Bread Lines in Germany at the end of World War 1. Even after the November 11 1911 armistice the Allies UK France USA maintained a food blockade to keep Germany in a submissive position. c. 1918-19 / Everett Collection / Bridgeman Images.

With thanks to The Academy of Political Science for permission to use the extract on page 20 from "Adenauer and a Crisis in Weimar Democracy" by Fritz Stern, vol 73, no.1, 1958, page 2.

Extract used on page 25 from The Weimar Republic by Eberhard Kolb, page 97. Published by Routledge, 2008.

Image used on page 27: German National Socialist / Universal History Archive/UIG / Bridgeman Images.

Extract used on page 31 from Hindenburg Power, Myth and the Rise of the Nazis by Anna von der Goltz. © Anna von der Goltz 2009. Reproduced with permission of the Licensor through PLSclear.

Extract used on page 31 republished with permission of Princeton University Press, from Weimar Germany: Promise and Tragedy, Weimar Centennial Edition by Eric D. Weitz, p. xviii. Copyright © 2007; permission conveyed through Copyright Clearance Center, Inc.

With thanks to Elliott & Thompson for permission to use the extracts on pages 32 and 33 from "Travellers in the Third Reich: The rise of fascism through the eyes of everyday people" by Julia Boyd.

Extract used on page 33 from THE "HITLER MYTH": IMAGE AND REALITY IN THE THIRD REICH by Ian Kershaw. Copyright © Ian Kershaw, 1987, used by permission of The Wylie Agency (UK) Limited.

Extracts used on pages 35 and 56 from A Concise History of Germany by Mary Fulbrook. © Cambridge University Press 1990. Reproduced with permission of the Licensor through PLSclear.

Extracts from An International History: Europe Since 1870 by James Joll on pages 39 and 49 reprinted by permission of Peters Fraser and Dunlop (www.petersfraserdunlop.com) on behalf of the Estate of James Joll.

With thanks to Pavilion Books for permission to use the extract on page 39 from Inside Nazi Germany: Conformity, Opposition and Racism in Everyday Life by Detlev J.K. Peukert.

With thanks to Oliver Pretzel and David Brandt for permission to use the extract on page 43 from "Germany: Jekyll & Hyde: An Eye Witness Analysis of Nazi Germany" by Sebastian Haffner.

Extracts used on pages 45 and 55 from "What We Knew: Terror, Mass Murder and Everyday Life in Nazi Germany" by Eric Johnson and Karl-Heinz Reuband. © 2005 by Eric A. Johnson and Karl-Heinz Reuband. Reproduced by John Murray Press, a division of Hodder and Stoughton Limited.

Image used on page 45: Der Schnueffler (The snooper) by A. Paul Weber, 1940 (b/w photo) / © SZ Photo / Scherl / Bridgeman Images.

With thanks to Dover Publications for permission to use the extract on page 52 from 'School for Barbarians' by Erika Mann.

Image used on page 53: Colour Hitler Youth poster from the Second World War / Universal History Archive/UIG / Bridgeman Images.

Extract used on page 55 from Between Dignity and Despair: Jewish Life in Nazi Germany by Marion Kaplan. Copyright © 1998 by Marion A. Kaplan. Reproduced with permission of the Licensor through PLSclear.

Extract used on page 56 from A/AS Level History for AQA Democracy and Nazism: Germany, 1918-1945 by Nick Pinfield. © Cambridge University Press 2015. Reproduced with permission of the Licensor through PLSclear.

Extract used on page 60 from "A Child of Hitler" by Alfons Heck, original copyright 1985, Renaissance House Publishers, Phoenix, Arizona USA.

With thanks to PNAS for permission to use the extract on page 60 from "Nazi indoctrination and anti-Semitic beliefs in Germany" by Nico Voigtländer and Hans-Joachim Voth. Article from "Proceedings of the National Academy of Sciences of the United States of America", Volume 112, No. 26 (June 30, 2015).

ISBN: 978 1 78908 287 6
Printed by Elanders Ltd, Newcastle upon Tyne.
Clipart from Corel®

Based on the classic CGP style created by Richard Parsons.

Contents

Exam Skills

Exam Hints and Tips

GCSE Edexcel History is made up of three papers. The papers test different skills and each one covers different topics. This page gives you more information about each exam so you'll know what to expect.

You will take 3 Papers altogether

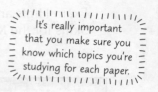

It's really important that you make sure you know which topics you're studying for each paper.

Paper 1 covers the Thematic Study and the Historic Environment

1) Paper 1 is 1 hour 15 minutes long. It's worth 52 marks — 30% of your GCSE.
   This paper will be divided into two sections:
   - Section A: Historic Environment.
   - Section B: Thematic Study.

Paper 2 covers the Period Study and the British Depth Study

2) Paper 2 is 1 hour 45 minutes long. It's worth 64 marks — 40% of your GCSE.
   This paper will be divided into two question and answer booklets:
   - Booklet P: Period Study.
   - Booklet B: British Depth Study.

Paper 3 covers the Modern Depth Study

This book covers the Modern Depth Study Weimar and Nazi Germany, 1918-39

3) Paper 3 is 1 hour 20 minutes long. It's worth 52 marks — 30% of your GCSE.
   This paper will be divided into two sections,
   both about the Modern Depth Study.
   - Section A: two questions — one is source-based and the other is an essay question.
   - Section B: a four-part question based around two sources and two interpretations.

Organise your Time in the exam

1) Always double check that you know how much time you have for each paper.
2) Learn the rule — the more marks a question is worth, the longer your answer should be.
   The number of marks available for each question is clearly shown in the exam paper.
3) Don't get carried away writing loads for a question that's only worth four marks
   — you need to leave time for the higher mark questions.
4) Try to leave a few minutes at the end of the exam to go back and read over your answers.

Always use a Clear Writing Style

1) Try to use clear handwriting — and pay attention to spelling, grammar and punctuation.
2) If you make a mistake, miss out a word or need to add extra information to a point, make your
   changes neatly. Check that the examiner will still be able to easily read and understand your answer.
3) Remember to start a new paragraph for each new point you want to discuss.
4) A brief introduction and conclusion will help to give structure to your essay
   answers and make sure you stay focused on the question.

Exam Hints and Tips

Remember these Tips for Approaching the Questions

Stay focused on the question

- Read the questions <u>carefully</u>. Underline the <u>key words</u>, so you know exactly what you need to do.
- Make sure that you <u>directly answer the question</u>. Don't just chuck in everything you know about the period.
- You've got to be <u>relevant</u> and <u>accurate</u> — make sure you include <u>precise details</u> like the <u>dates</u> of <u>important events</u> in the history of Nazi Germany and the <u>names</u> of the people who were <u>involved</u>.
- It might help to try to write the <u>first sentence</u> of every <u>paragraph</u> in a way that <u>addresses</u> the question, e.g. "Another reason why there was a revolution in Germany in 1918 was..."

Plan your essay answers

- You <u>don't</u> need to plan answers to the <u>shorter questions</u> in the exam.
- For <u>longer essay questions</u>, it's very important to make a <u>quick plan</u> before you start writing. This will help to make your answer <u>well organised</u> and <u>structured</u>, with each point <u>leading clearly</u> to your <u>conclusion</u>.
- Look at the <u>key words</u> in the question. Scribble a <u>quick plan</u> of your <u>main points</u> — <u>cross through this neatly</u> at the end, so it's obvious it shouldn't be marked.

Modern Depth Studies include questions about Sources...

1) Sources are pieces of <u>evidence from the period</u> you're studying — such as a <u>newspaper cartoon</u> criticising the Weimar Republic or an extract from a <u>speech</u> made by Hitler.

2) Sources may also be someone's <u>reflections</u> on an issue or event they experienced, written or recorded after it took place. For example, a source could be an <u>interview</u> with someone who lived in Nazi Germany, recorded several years after the end of the Second World War.

3) Historians use sources to <u>find out</u> about and <u>make sense</u> of the past. They have to choose sources <u>carefully</u> to make sure they're <u>useful</u> for the specific question they are trying to answer.

4) Once they find a useful source, they use it to arrive at <u>conclusions</u> about the topic they're studying — this is called <u>making inferences</u>.

... and Interpretations

1) <u>Interpretations</u> are written by <u>historians</u>. They express <u>opinions</u> about an event or issue in the past. For example, an interpretation could be an extract from a <u>textbook</u> or a <u>biography</u>.

2) Historians study <u>sources</u> when they're writing <u>interpretations</u> — sources help them to understand the past and develop their <u>point of view</u>.

3) <u>Different historians</u> might come up with <u>different interpretations</u> of the <u>same topic</u>. There are lots of reasons why this might happen:

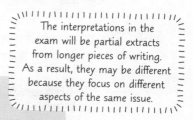

The interpretations in the exam will be partial extracts from longer pieces of writing. As a result, they may be different because they focus on different aspects of the same issue.

- They might have used <u>different sources</u> when doing their research.
- They may disagree over <u>how important</u> a particular source is.
- They may have <u>different opinions</u> about how <u>significant</u> a <u>certain event</u> was.

Learn this page and make exam stress history...

Jotting down a quick plan of the different points you're going to make before you start writing can really help you to make sure your answer is clearly written and has a nice logical structure.

Skills for the Modern Depth Study

These two pages will give you some advice on how to approach the Modern Depth Study, as well as how to find your way around this book. Activity types are colour-coded to help you find what you need.

The Modern Depth Study tests Four different Skills

1) Throughout the Modern Depth Study, you'll be expected to show your knowledge and understanding of the topic, as well as your ability to apply historical concepts, such as cause and consequence.

2) For questions which ask you to analyse sources and interpretations you'll also need to use more specific skills.

3) The activities in this book will help you to practise all the different skills you'll need for the exam.

Source Analysis

1) Question 1 in the exam will ask you to infer two things from a source.

> Infer two things from Source A about German society at the end of the First World War. Explain each inference that you make. [4 marks]

2) When answering this question, it's important that you don't just describe what you can see or read in the source. You need to read between the lines to draw conclusions about the aspect of Weimar and Nazi Germany given in the question.

3) Question 3(a) will ask you to consider how useful two sources are for a particular investigation.

> Explain how useful Sources B and C are for an investigation into the reasons for Hitler's popularity. Use both sources, as well as your own knowledge, to support your answer. [8 marks]

4) For each source, you should think about:
   - The date — when the source was produced
   - The author — who produced it
   - The purpose — why it might have been produced
   - The content — what the source says or shows

5) In your answer, you need to explain how these factors affect the usefulness of the source for the investigation given in the question.

> For example, this poster of Hitler is useful for an investigation into the reasons for Hitler's popularity because it's a Nazi propaganda poster, so it provides evidence of how the Nazis presented Hitler to the public. This can help us to understand why some Germans supported him.

6) You may be given both written and visual sources, but you should handle them both in the same way.

> The Source Analysis activities in this book will help you to practise understanding sources, making inferences from them and analysing their usefulness.

Ein Volk, ein Reich, ein Führer!

© Mary Evans / Sueddeutsche Zeitung Photo

Skills for the Modern Depth Study

Interpretation

1) Questions 3(b), (c) and (d) focus on two interpretations which give different views on the same subject.

2) For question 3(b), you'll have to identify the main difference between the two views.

3) Question 3(c) will ask you to explain why you think the interpretations give different views. Think about whether they focus on different areas of the topic, or rely on different sources. You can use the two sources given for question 3(a) to support your answer.

4) For question 3(d), you'll have to explain how far you agree with one of the interpretations. Decide your opinion before you start writing, and state it clearly at the beginning and end of your answer. You need to discuss arguments both for and against the view given in the interpretation, using the other interpretation and your own knowledge to support your answer.

> The Interpretation activities in this book will help you to compare interpretations and use them to write a clear, well-structured argument.

> Interpretations 1 and 2 give different opinions about the extent of opposition to the Nazis in the years 1933-39. Explain the main difference between these opinions. [4 marks]

> Give one reason why these interpretations give different opinions. [4 marks]

> Explain how far you agree with Interpretation 1 about the extent of opposition to the Nazis in the years 1933-39. [20 marks]

Knowledge and Understanding

Although you'll be given sources and interpretations in the exam, you'll need to use your own knowledge and understanding of the topic to back up your answers. This is especially important for questions 2, 3(a) and 3(d).

> The Knowledge and Understanding activities in this book will help you to revise key features and events from the period — what was happening, when it was happening, who was involved and all the other important details.

Thinking Historically

1) As well as knowing what happened when, you also need to use historical concepts to analyse key events and developments. These concepts include continuity and change, cause and consequence, similarity and difference, and significance.

2) Question 2 will ask you to explain the causes of a key event or issue. You need to back up every point you make with evidence and explain why the evidence illustrates the point you're making.

> The Thinking Historically activities in this book will help you to practise using historical concepts to analyse different parts of the topic.

> Explain why Hitler became Chancellor of Germany in January 1933. [12 marks]

Modern history — remembering what you did yesterday...

Dealing with sources and interpretations might seem tricky at first, but don't worry — this book is crammed with useful questions and activities to help you practise all the skills you need.

The Weimar Republic, 1918-29

The War Ends

World War I lasted from 1914-1918. Fighting ended with the armistice on November 11th 1918. By this time, Germany was experiencing widespread unrest, which eventually resulted in a revolution.

The war was Devastating for Germany

1) Near the war's end, German people were suffering severe hardship.
2) The Allies had set up naval blockades which prevented imports of food and essential goods. By 1918, many people faced starvation.
3) Public opinion turned against Kaiser Wilhelm II, who ruled the German Empire like a king. Many Germans wanted a democracy and an end to the war — there was widespread unrest.

A British cartoon from 1917. German civilians queue for food as an over-fed official walks past them. The cartoonist is highlighting the difference between the lifestyle of Germany's rich officers and that of the rest of its struggling population.

- In early November 1918 some members of the German navy rebelled and refused to board their ships.
- In Hanover, German troops refused to control rioters.
- A Jewish communist called Kurt Eisner encouraged a general uprising, which sparked mass strikes in Munich.

Social Unrest turned into Revolution

1) By November 1918, the situation in Germany verged on civil war. A huge public protest was held in Berlin, and members of the SPD (Social Democratic Party) called for the Kaiser's resignation.

2) Kaiser Wilhelm abdicated (resigned) on 9th November 1918. On the same day, two different socialist parties — the Social Democratic Party and the Independent Social Democratic Party (USPD) — declared a republic.

> A republic is a country ruled without a monarch (king or queen) — power is held by the people via elected representatives.

3) On November 10th, all the state leaders that had been appointed by the monarchy left their posts. New revolutionary state governments took over instead. The monarchy had been abolished and Germany had the chance to become a democracy.

> Germany was made up of 18 states, and each had its own government. The national government decided national affairs, and state governments dealt with more local affairs.

The signing of the armistice

- On 11th November 1918, a ceasefire to end the First World War was agreed. The Allies (Britain, France and the USA) signed an armistice (truce) with Germany.
- The new republic was under pressure to sign. The government didn't think Germany could continue fighting — its people were starving and military morale was low.
- The armistice wasn't supported by some right-wing Germans, who saw the truce as a betrayal. They believed Germany could still win the war.

The Socialists set up a Temporary Government

1) After the abdication of the Kaiser, Germany was disorganised. Different political parties claimed control over different towns.
2) A temporary national government was established, consisting of the SPD and the USPD. It was called the Council of People's Representatives.
3) It controlled Germany until January 1919, when elections were held for a new Reichstag (parliament) — see p.8.

The War Ends

Now that you know all about the end of the war in Germany, you need to make sure you can use your knowledge to explain exactly how Germany's various problems contributed to the Revolution of 1918.

Knowledge and Understanding

1) Use the information on the previous page to write a definition for each of the following:

   a) The SPD and the USPD   d) State governments

   b) Kaiser Wilhelm II   e) Armistice

   c) Republic   f) The Council of People's Representatives

2) Knowing the order that events happened in is essential if you want to understand a topic well. Copy and complete the timeline below by filling in all the key events between November 1918 and January 1919. Include as much detail as you can.

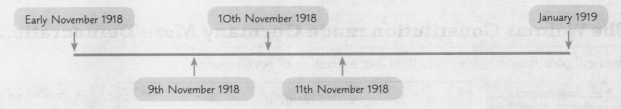

Early November 1918   10th November 1918   January 1919

9th November 1918   11th November 1918

Thinking Historically

1) In the exam, you might be asked to explain the causes of a particular event or movement. Using your knowledge of the social, economic and political conditions in Germany in 1918, copy and complete the table below, explaining how each factor contributed to the Revolution.

Factor	How it contributed to the Revolution
a) **Allied naval blockades**	
b) **Attitudes towards Kaiser Wilhelm**	
c) **Disobedience in the army and the navy**	
d) **Kurt Eisner**	

2) Which of the factors above do you think was the most important cause of the Revolution? Write a few sentences to explain your answer.

To decide whether one factor is more or less important than another, it's useful to consider how many other factors it's linked to. The most important factors are usually linked to several others.

EXAM TIP

Revolutions pop up in history over and over again...

Remember to keep your answers focused on the question given to you — at the end of each paragraph it's a good idea to spell out exactly how the point you've made answers the question.

The Weimar Republic, 1918-29

The Weimar Republic

The Weimar Republic was the first time Germany had ever been governed as a democracy. It was designed to give the German people a voice. However, there were major flaws in its constitution that made it weak.

The Weimar Republic was formed

1) The Council of People's Representatives organised elections in January 1919 to create a new parliament. Germany was now a democracy — the people would say how the country was run.

2) Friedrich Ebert became the first President, with Philip Scheidemann as Chancellor. Ebert was leader of the SPD, a moderate party of socialists.

3) In February 1919, the members of the new Reichstag (parliament) met at Weimar to create a new constitution for Germany. Historians call this period of Germany's history the Weimar Republic.

> The constitution decided how the government would be organised, and established its main principles.

The Weimar Constitution made Germany More Democratic...

The new constitution reorganised the German system of government.

> Proportional representation is where the proportion of seats a party wins in parliament is roughly the same as the proportion of the total votes they win.

President
- Elected every 7 years.
- Chooses the Chancellor and is head of the army.
- Can dissolve the Reichstag, call new elections and suspend the constitution.

> The President was elected by the German people, and so were the parties in the Reichstag. The President had the most power, but the Chancellor was in charge of the day-to-day running of government.

Reichstag
- The new German parliament.
- Members are elected every 4 years using proportional representation.

Reichsrat
- Second (less powerful) house of parliament.
- Consists of members from each local region.
- Can delay measures passed by the Reichstag.

1) The new constitution was designed to be as fair as possible. Even very small political parties were given seats in the Reichstag if they got 0.4% of the vote or above.

2) The constitution allowed women to vote for the first time, and lowered the voting age to 20 — more Germans could vote and the German public had greater power.

...but the Constitution had Weaknesses

Even though the new constitution was more democratic, it didn't prove to be very efficient.

1) Proportional representation meant that even parties with a very small number of votes were guaranteed to get into the Reichstag. This meant it was difficult to make decisions because there were so many parties, and they all had different points of view.

2) When a decision couldn't be reached, the President could suspend the constitution and pass laws without the Reichstag's consent.

> The President's ability to force through his own decision was known as 'Article 48'.

3) This power was only supposed to be used in an emergency, but became a useful way of getting around disagreements that took place in the Reichstag. This meant it undermined the new democracy.

The Weimar Republic

SKILLS PRACTICE

The activities on this page focus on the balance between the Weimar Constitution's strengths and weaknesses.

Thinking Historically

1) The table below lists four features of the Weimar Constitution.
Tick the relevant box to show whether each feature was a strength of the
Constitution, a weakness, or both. Give an explanation for each choice.

Feature of the Constitution	Strength	Weakness	Both
a) **Members of the Reichstag elected by proportional representation**			
b) **Any party with more than 0.4% of the vote gets seats in the Reichstag**			
c) **Women and younger people allowed to vote**			
d) **The President has emergency powers to overrule the Reichstag**			

Interpretation

This extract is from a study of Weimar and Nazi Germany by William L. Shirer, published in 1961.

1) Read the interpretation, then answer the questions in the pink boxes.

a) What features of the Weimar Constitution made it 'liberal and democratic'?

The constitution which emerged from the Assembly after six months of debate... was, on paper, the most liberal* and democratic document of its kind the twentieth century had seen... full of ingenious and admirable devices which seemed to guarantee the working of an almost flawless democracy... No man in the world would be more free than a German, no government more democratic and liberal than his. On paper at least.

*allowing people a lot of freedom

b) Why do you think Shirer stresses that the Weimar Constitution worked 'on paper'?

2) Write a brief summary of Shirer's main argument. What does he suggest was good about the Weimar Constitution? Does he think it was as good in practice as it seemed in theory?

3) Using your table of strengths and weaknesses above to help you, explain how far you agree with Shirer's main argument about the Weimar Constitution.

EXAM TIP

The Weimar Republic was vulnerable from the beginning...
When you're facing a tricky interpretation, there are a few things you can do to make your life easier. Try tackling the interpretation one sentence at a time, underlining key words as you go.

Early Unpopularity

The Treaty of Versailles was signed in June 1919. The treaty was very unpopular in Germany and many Germans resented the new government for accepting its terms — not exactly a great start for the Republic.

Ebert signed the Treaty of Versailles

1) After the armistice, a peace treaty called the Treaty of Versailles was imposed on Germany.

2) The terms of the treaty were mostly decided by the Allied leaders — David Lloyd George (Britain), Georges Clemenceau (France) and Woodrow Wilson (USA).

Comment and Analysis

As a result, the Weimar Republic became associated with the pain and humiliation caused by the Treaty of Versailles.

The new German government wasn't invited to the peace conference in 1919 and had no say in the Versailles Treaty. At first, Ebert refused to sign the treaty, but in the end he had little choice — Germany was too weak to risk restarting the conflict. In June 1919, he accepted its terms and signed.

The Terms of the Versailles Treaty were Severe

1) Article 231 of the treaty said Germany had to take the blame for the war — the War-Guilt Clause.

Many Germans didn't agree with this, and were humiliated by having to accept total blame.

2) Germany's armed forces were reduced to 100,000 men. They weren't allowed any armoured vehicles, aircraft or submarines, and could only have 6 warships.

This made Germans feel vulnerable.

3) Germany was forced to pay £6600 million in reparations — payments for the damage caused by German forces in the war. The amount was decided in 1921 but was changed later.

The heavy reparations seemed unfair to Germans and would cause lasting damage to Germany's economy.

4) Germany lost its empire — areas around the world that used to belong to Germany were now called mandates. They were put under the control of countries on the winning side of the war by the League of Nations — an organisation which aimed to settle international disputes peacefully.

People opposed the losses in territory, especially when people in German colonies were forced to become part of a new nation.

5) The German military was banned from the Rhineland — an area of Germany on its western border with France. This left Germany open to attack from the west.

Germany Felt Betrayed by the Weimar Republic

The Treaty of Versailles caused resentment towards the Weimar Republic.

1) Germans called the treaty a 'Diktat' (a treaty forced upon Germany), and many blamed Ebert for accepting its terms.

The Weimar politicians involved in signing the armistice became known as the 'November Criminals'.

2) Some Germans believed the armistice was a mistake and that Germany could have won the war. They felt 'stabbed in the back' by the Weimar politicians, who brought the Treaty of Versailles upon Germany unnecessarily.

Comment and Analysis

The Treaty of Versailles played an important part in the failure of the Weimar Republic. It harmed the Republic's popularity, and created economic and political unrest that hindered the government for years.

© Mary Evans Picture Library

This German cartoon demonstrates Germany's feelings towards the Treaty of Versailles. The Allies are shown as demons, out for revenge.

Early Unpopularity

Use this page to test your knowledge of the Treaty of Versailles and people's attitudes towards it.

Knowledge and Understanding

One of the best revision techniques for something like the Treaty of Versailles is to make flashcards. They'll make it quick and easy for you to test yourself whenever you want to refresh your memory.

1) Make a flashcard for each term of the Treaty of Versailles on the previous page. On one side, write down the term's details. On the other side, explain why it was unpopular in Germany.

2) Why did the politicians who signed the treaty become known as the 'November Criminals'?

Source Analysis

Look at the source below. It is a German cartoon published after Germany signed the Treaty of Versailles. The cartoon is called 'The Future of Germany'. It shows the Allied countries (Britain, France and the USA) squeezing reparations payments out of Germany.

a) The Allies outnumber Germany and look bigger and stronger.

b) The title of the cartoon is 'The Future of Germany'.

c) Germany is being wrung out by the Allied countries.

d) The Allies are collecting the money that they're squeezing out of Germany.

© INTERFOTO / Alamy Stock Photo

1) Explain what you can infer from each detail in the blue boxes above. You may be able to make more than one inference from some of the details. An example is given below.

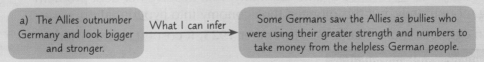

a) The Allies outnumber Germany and look bigger and stronger.

What I can infer

Some Germans saw the Allies as bullies who were using their greater strength and numbers to take money from the helpless German people.

EXAM TIP

Germans felt 'stabbed in the back' by the government...

The first question in the exam will ask you to infer two things from a source. To get full marks, you'll need to back up each inference that you make with a specific detail from the source.

Years of Unrest

The first four years of the Weimar Republic (1919-1923) were dominated by political, social and economic unrest. It created hardship for the German people, and fuelled criticism of Ebert's government.

There was Widespread Discontent in Germany

1) By 1919, thousands of Germans were poor and starving, and an influenza epidemic had killed thousands.
2) Many Germans denied they had lost the war and blamed the 'November Criminals' who had agreed to the armistice and the Treaty of Versailles.
3) Others who were blamed for losing the war included communists and Jews.
4) The government was seen as weak and ineffective — the Treaty of Versailles made living conditions worse.

Soon there were Riots and Rebellions

The government faced threats from left-wing and right-wing political groups.

The extreme left wanted a revolution...
- In January 1919, communists led by Karl Liebknecht and Rosa Luxemburg tried to take over Berlin. They took control of important buildings like newspaper headquarters, and 50,000 workers went on strike in support of the left-wing revolution. This became known as the Spartacist Revolt.
- Ebert asked for help from the right-wing Freikorps (ex-German soldiers) to stop the rebellion. Over 100 workers were killed. The Freikorps' use of violence caused a split on the left between the Social Democratic Party and the communists.

The right also rebelled against the Weimar government...
- In March 1920, some of the Freikorps themselves took part in the Kapp Putsch ('Putsch' means revolt) — led by Wolfgang Kapp. They wanted to create a new right-wing government.
- The Freikorps marched into Berlin to overthrow the Weimar regime. But German workers opposed the putsch and staged a general strike. Berlin was paralysed and Kapp was forced to give up.
- Even after the putsch failed, threats to the government remained. In 1922, some former Freikorps members assassinated Walter Rathenau — he'd been Foreign Minister and was Jewish. ◄

> As Germany's economic problems got worse after the war, anti-Semitic (anti-Jewish) feelings increased.

In 1923 Germany Couldn't Pay its Reparations

1) By 1923, Germany could no longer meet the reparations payments set out by the Treaty of Versailles.
2) France and Belgium decided to take Germany's resources instead, so they occupied the Ruhr — the richest industrial part of Germany. This gave them access to Germany's iron and coal reserves. The occupation led to fury in Germany, and caused a huge strike in the Ruhr.
3) German industry was devastated again. Germany tried to solve her debt problem by printing more money, but this plunged the economy into hyperinflation. ◄

> Hyperinflation happens when production can't keep up with the amount of money in circulation, so the money keeps losing its value.

4) In 1918, an egg cost ¼ of a Mark. By November 1923, it cost 80 million Marks.

The consequences of hyperinflation
- Germany's currency became worthless. Nobody wanted to trade with Germany, so shortages of food and goods got worse.
- Bank savings also became worthless. The hardest hit were the middle classes.

> By 1923, even basic necessities were hard to get hold of. The German people were undergoing immense hardship, which they'd now come to associate with the rise of the Weimar Republic.

Years of Unrest

We covered a lot on the last page, so have a go at these activities to make sure it's all sunk in.

Knowledge and Understanding

1) For each of the following people or groups, write a few lines to explain who they were and what they did in the early years of the Weimar Republic.

   a) Karl Liebknecht and Rosa Luxemburg   b) The Freikorps   c) Wolfgang Kapp

Interpretation

The interpretation below is from a book by British author Geoff Layton, published in 2009.

> The extent of the opposition from the extreme right to democracy was not always appreciated*. Instead, President Ebert and the Weimar governments overestimated the threat from the extreme left and they came to rely on the forces of reaction for justice and law and order... the danger of the extreme right was actually insidious**; it was the real growing threat to Weimar democracy.

*fully understood   **growing slowly, but very harmful

1) What does the author suggest was the biggest threat to Weimar democracy? Find a detail from the text that supports your answer.

2) Give three pieces of evidence from your own knowledge to support each of the arguments below. Explain how each piece of evidence supports the argument.

   a) The greatest threat to the Weimar Republic came from the right.
   b) The greatest threat to the Weimar Republic came from the left.

Thinking Historically

1) The flowchart below is about hyperinflation in Weimar Germany. Copy and complete the flowchart, adding the consequences of each event. Try to include as much detail as possible.

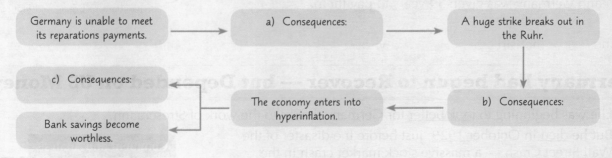

Hyperinflation — sounds good for blowing up balloons...

If you're struggling to understand the causes or consequences of a particular event, drawing a flowchart might help you. It's a fantastic way to make sense of how one thing led to another.

The Weimar Republic, 1918-29

Recovery

In 1923, Gustav Stresemann became <u>Chancellor</u> of the Weimar Republic. His <u>domestic</u> and <u>international</u> policies helped the German economy to recover, resulting in the '<u>Golden Years</u>' of the Weimar Republic.

Stresemann introduced a New Currency

1) Gustav Stresemann was <u>Chancellor</u> of the Weimar Republic between <u>August</u> and <u>November 1923</u>. He made important changes to help Germany to recover from its economic crisis.

2) In September 1923, he <u>ended the strike</u> in the Ruhr. This <u>reduced tension</u> between Germany, France and Belgium, and meant the government could stop <u>compensation payments</u> to strikers.

3) In November 1923, Stresemann replaced the German Mark with the <u>Rentenmark</u> to stabilise Germany's currency.

4) Stresemann created the '<u>great coalition</u>' — a group of moderate, pro-democracy socialist parties in the Reichstag who agreed to <u>work together</u>. This allowed parliament to make decisions <u>more quickly</u>.

Stresemann wanted International Cooperation

In November 1923, Stresemann became <u>Foreign Minister</u>. He tried to cooperate more with other countries and build better <u>international relationships</u>. Germany's economy prospered as a result.

1) **The Dawes Plan** was signed in 1924. Stresemann secured France and Belgium's <u>withdrawal</u> from the <u>Ruhr</u> and agreed more <u>realistic</u> payment dates for the reparations. The USA <u>lent</u> Germany £40 million to help it pay off its other debts.

2) **The Locarno Pact** was signed in October 1925. Germany, France and Belgium agreed to respect their <u>joint borders</u> — even those created as a result of the Treaty of Versailles.

3) **The League of Nations** (see p.10) allowed Germany to join in <u>1926</u>. Germany was <u>re-established</u> as an international power.

4) **The Kellogg-Briand Pact** was signed by Germany in 1928, alongside 65 other countries. They promised <u>not</u> to use <u>violence</u> to settle disputes.

5) **The Young Plan** was agreed in 1929. The Allies agreed to <u>reduce</u> the reparations to a <u>quarter</u> of the original amount, and Germany was given <u>59 years</u> to pay them.

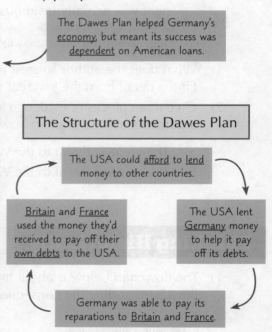

The Dawes Plan helped Germany's <u>economy</u>, but meant its success was <u>dependent</u> on American loans.

The Structure of the Dawes Plan

The USA could <u>afford</u> to <u>lend</u> money to other countries.

<u>Britain</u> and <u>France</u> used the money they'd received to pay off their <u>own debts</u> to the USA.

The USA lent <u>Germany</u> money to help it pay off its debts.

Germany was able to pay its reparations to <u>Britain</u> and <u>France</u>.

Germany had begun to Recover — but Depended on US Money

1) Life was beginning to <u>look better</u> for Germany thanks to the work of Stresemann.

2) But he <u>died</u> in October <u>1929</u>, just before the disaster of the <u>Wall Street Crash</u> — a massive stock market crash in the USA which started a global economic depression.

3) The plans he had agreed would only work if the <u>USA</u> had <u>enough money</u> to keep lending to Germany — but after the crash, it didn't. Things were suddenly going to <u>get worse again</u> (see p.26).

Comment and Analysis

Germany's economic recovery helped <u>restore faith</u> in the Weimar Republic — there was strong support for pro-Weimar political parties in the <u>1928 elections</u>.

Recovery

Try your hand at these activities, which focus on Stresemann's impact on German politics and economics.

Knowledge and Understanding

1) Copy and complete this table about the agreements made by Germany from 1924 to 1929.

Agreement	Year	What was agreed?
a) **Dawes Plan**		
b) **Locarno Pact**		
c) **League of Nations**		
d) **Kellogg-Briand Pact**		
e) **Young Plan**		

2) Explain why these agreements helped to make Germany more stable.

Source Analysis

The source below comes from a speech made by Foreign Minister Gustav Stresemann to the League of Nations, shortly before his death in 1929.

> Germany's capacity* to pay is overestimated abroad. Germany gives a false impression of prosperity**. The economic position is flourishing only on the surface. Germany is in fact dancing on a volcano. If the short-term credits (foreign loans) are called in, a large section of our economy will collapse.

*ability   **wealth

1) Imagine you're going to use this source for an investigation into Germany's economic recovery between 1923 and 1929. Copy and complete the mind map below by explaining how each feature of the source affects its usefulness for your investigation.

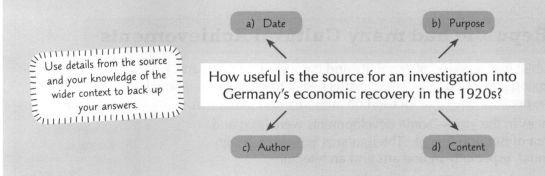

Use details from the source and your knowledge of the wider context to back up your answers.

a) Date   b) Purpose

How useful is the source for an investigation into Germany's economic recovery in the 1920s?

c) Author   d) Content

No need to Strese, mann — it's all under control...

Don't forget to think about the purpose of a source. Why was it created? Who was intended to read it or see it? What impression might the author or illustrator be trying to create?

The Weimar Republic, 1918-29

Changes Under the Weimar Republic

Despite political, social and economic unrest, life did improve for some under the Weimar Republic.

Living standards Improved for the Working Classes

During the 'Golden Years', living standards improved in the Weimar Republic. This was a result of Germany's economic prosperity, but also of the reforms which took place throughout the 1920s.

What Improved	How It Improved
Unemployment	The unemployed were more protected. In 1927 the government introduced unemployment insurance. Workers could pay into the scheme and would receive cash benefits if they became unemployed.
Wages	The working classes became more prosperous. Wages for industrial workers rose quickly in the late 1920s.
Housing	The government launched mass housing projects. More than 2 million new homes were built between 1924 and 1931. This also provided extra employment.

Comment and Analysis

Not everyone benefited from higher standards of living. The middle classes felt ignored by the Weimar government and their resentment made it easier for the government's political opponents to gain support.

Despite these changes, some problems remained:

1) Higher living standards could only be maintained with a strong economy, and Germany's was fragile.
2) The changes mainly helped the working classes — the middle classes couldn't access the welfare benefits.

Women gained more Freedoms

Women were given more freedom and greater access to public life under the Weimar Republic.

1) Politically, women were given more representation. They were awarded the vote and could enter politics more easily — between 1919 and 1932, 112 women were elected to the Reichstag.

2) Women showed that they were capable workers during the war, and the number of young women working increased.

3) The traditional role of women began to change. New female sports clubs and societies sprang up, and women had more opportunities.

4) Divorce became easier, and the number of divorces rose.

Comment and Analysis

These changes fuelled right-wing criticism — some German nationalists thought giving women more power and freedom threatened traditional family life and values in Germany.

The Weimar Republic had many Cultural Achievements

1) The Weimar Republic was a period of creativity and innovation in Germany. Freedom of expression generated new ideas. Artists began to question traditional forms and styles, especially ones that focused on authority and militarism.

2) There were advances in the arts — some developments were bold and new, like the drama of Bertholt Brecht. The Bauhaus School of design was highly influential, especially in fine arts and architecture.

3) There were also important changes in music, literature and cinema. German films were successful — e.g. 'Metropolis' directed by Fritz Lang.

4) The Weimar Republic encouraged new ways of critical thinking at places like Frankfurt University, and a cabaret culture developed in Berlin.

Not all Germans liked the rejection of traditional forms and values in Weimar culture. Some were afraid it symbolised a loss of German tradition.

Changes Under the Weimar Republic

The Weimar Republic had its ups as well as its downs. This has made it hard for historians to agree about how much things really changed for the better — let's take a look at different ways of assessing it.

Interpretation

Interpretation 1

It is estimated that workers' real wages increased by 9% in 1927 and by a further 12% in 1928, making the German labour force the highest paid industrial work force in Europe... At the same time, their living standards were raised by a steady expansion in municipal house-building programmes, improvements in health care and a steady growth in welfare provision. Between 1924 and 1931, just over 2 million new homes were built, and a further 195 000 modernised.

An extract from a book by Ruth Henig, published in 1998.

Interpretation 2

And there were yet other clouds on the Weimar horizon... the economy was heavily dependent on US loans... unemployment never fell below 1.3 million. And even before the crisis of 1929, support for middle-of-the-road parties was declining as many middle-class voters felt that Stresemann's foreign policy successes had little positive impact on their local economy and wellbeing. The Weimar Republic was therefore much more vulnerable than it appeared.

An extract from a book by Martyn Whittock, published in 2011.

1) Which aspects of life in Weimar Germany does each interpretation focus on?
2) What evidence does each author use to support their interpretation?
3) Which of the two interpretations gives a more positive view about the Weimar Republic? Why do you think this is? Use your answers to questions 1 and 2 to help you.

Knowledge and Understanding

1) Copy and complete the mind map below about how living conditions improved during the 'Golden Years' of the Weimar Republic. For each heading, add ways in which it improved.

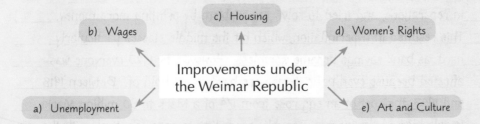

b) Wages   c) Housing   d) Women's Rights

Improvements under the Weimar Republic

a) Unemployment   e) Art and Culture

2) Using your completed mind map to help you, explain why the years from 1924 to 1929 are often seen as the 'Golden Years' of the Weimar Republic.

It wasn't all doom and gloom...

When you're writing a longer exam answer, it's important to link your ideas together clearly. Use linking words and phrases like 'for example', 'therefore', 'because of this' and 'however'.

The Weimar Republic, 1918-29

Worked Exam-Style Question

This sample answer will give you an idea of how to write an answer that explains causation.

Explain why the Weimar Republic was unpopular between 1919 and 1923.
You could mention reparations and political weaknesses in your answer, but you should also use your own knowledge.   [12 marks]

The prompts in the question are only there as a guide. To get a high mark, you'll also need to include ideas of your own that go beyond the prompts.

The Weimar Republic was very unpopular in Germany between 1919 and 1923. From the outset, many Germans distrusted its politicians because of their involvement in the 1918 Armistice, which ended the First World War. Some Germans felt betrayed by these 'November Criminals', as they thought Germany could have continued fighting and won the war. This undermined the popularity of the Weimar Republic before it had even begun.

Make sure your points are relevant to the question.

This links back to the question by explaining how this factor affected the Republic's popularity.

Another important cause of the Weimar Republic's unpopularity was President Ebert's decision to sign the Treaty of Versailles (June 1919). Many Germans were angry with President Ebert for accepting the treaty's conditions, which were seen as very unfair. Germany lost its empire, its military was significantly reduced and German forces were banned from the Rhineland, leaving Germany open to attack from the west. Germans also felt humiliated by Article 231, which forced Germany to accept total blame for the war. In the eyes of the German public, signing the Treaty of Versailles was a betrayal and a display of the Weimar Republic's weakness.

Giving specific examples shows you know the topic well.

The first sentence in each paragraph links back to the question.

The Weimar Republic was also unpopular because Germans came to associate it with the crippling reparations payments laid down in the Treaty of Versailles. Many Germans were living in poverty by 1919 and reparations placed huge financial pressure on Germany, making living conditions even worse. The government was unable to pay the £6600 million demanded in reparations, and tried to solve the problem by printing more money. This resulted in hyperinflation, which hit the middle classes particularly hard, as bank savings became worthless. However, by 1923 everyone was affected because even basic items were hard to get hold of. Between 1918 and 1923, the cost of an egg rose from 1/4 of a Mark to 80 million Marks. People blamed the Weimar Republic for failing to cope effectively with the consequences of the reparations.

This explains why reparations made the Republic unpopular.

Worked Exam-Style Question

The Weimar Republic's domestic political weaknesses also played a part in its unpopularity. The Weimar constitution introduced a system of proportional representation, which meant that lots of different parties were represented in the Reichstag. This often made the Reichstag slow to come to decisions, which frustrated the German public.

The Republic's political weakness fuelled political instability, which further harmed its popularity. The government was unable to stop the left-wing Spartacist Revolt (1919) on its own, so it had to rely on the help of the right-wing Freikorps to prevent it. In 1920, the Freikorps themselves attempted a coup, and in 1923 Hitler attempted to gain power in the Munich Putsch. Although these challenges were all unsuccessful, they created political instability in the Weimar Republic and emphasised the weaknesses of its government.

The Republic also had a reputation for being weak internationally when dealing with the Allies, which was made worse by its response to the French and Belgian invasion of the Ruhr in 1923. Many Germans were angry at the invasion and held a large strike in the Ruhr, but the government called the strike off. This made the government seem unpatriotic, as it appeared unwilling to defend Germany from further humiliation. Many Germans felt betrayed by the fact that the government didn't want to stand up for its country at a time when Germany was particularly vulnerable.

Think about how one factor might have affected another.

Including dates shows that you can provide accurate information.

It's important to include factors that weren't mentioned as prompts in the question.

Exam-Style Questions

The questions on these pages will help you practise answering exam questions about Weimar Germany.

Source A

A photograph showing a queue for bread rations in Germany near the end of the First World War.

Source B

An extract from Kaiser Wilhelm II's memoirs, written in 1922, while he was living in Holland. He is discussing his abdication.

> In this struggle, I set aside all that was personal. I consciously sacrificed myself and my throne in the belief that, by so doing, I was best serving the interests of my beloved fatherland. The sacrifice was in vain. My departure brought us neither better armistice conditions nor better peace terms; nor did it prevent civil war — on the contrary, it hastened and intensified... the disintegration of the army and the nation.

Interpretation 1

An extract from a journal article by historian Fritz Stern, published in 1958.

> Between 1924 and 1929, the Republic even enjoyed an apparent period of prosperity and stability... But even in its halcyon* days, the deep divisions, the hatreds, and the ensuing** political instability persisted. How feeble and divided Weimar really was... how the past and the future cast their shadows over Weimar's middle years and prevented the forming of any kind of political consensus***.

> *peaceful   **resulting   ***agreement

Exam-Style Questions

Interpretation 2

An interpretation about the stability of the Weimar Republic, written in 2018.

> Having survived a period of great political and economic unrest from 1919 to 1924, Weimar politicians made some progress in addressing many of Germany's most pressing problems in the latter half of the 1920s. Indeed, the increased support for democratic parties in the 1928 elections suggests that the Weimar Republic may well have continued to thrive if it weren't for the Wall Street Crash and the fierce energy of political opposition.

Exam-Style Questions

1) Explain how useful Sources A and B are for an investigation into the reasons behind Kaiser Wilhelm II's abdication in November 1918. Use both sources, as well as your own knowledge, to support your answer.   [8 marks]

2) Explain why the German economy experienced a recovery between 1924 and 1929. You could mention the Rentenmark and the Dawes Plan in your answer, but you should also use your own knowledge.   [12 marks]

3) Look at Interpretations 1 and 2, which give different opinions about the stability of the Weimar Republic in the years 1924-29. Explain the main difference between the two opinions.   [4 marks]

4) Give one reason why Interpretations 1 and 2 might express different opinions about the stability of the Weimar Republic in the years 1924-29.   [4 marks]

5) To what extent do you agree with the opinion expressed in Interpretation 1 about the stability of the Weimar Republic in the years 1924-29? You should use both interpretations and your own knowledge to support your answer.   [16 marks]

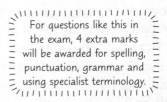
For questions like this in the exam, 4 extra marks will be awarded for spelling, punctuation, grammar and using specialist terminology.

Early Stages of the Nazi Party

Hitler entered German politics around the time the Weimar Republic was formed. By the time the Nazi Party was founded in 1920, he was growing in influence and became an opponent of the Weimar government.

Adolf Hitler became the Voice of the German Workers' Party

Hitler began his political career in the German Workers' Party — a nationalist party led by Anton Drexler.

1) Hitler joined the German Workers' Party in January 1919, when he was still in the German army. He became known for his talent as a passionate and skilled speaker, and crowds gathered to hear him talk.

> In 1919, the German Workers' Party had around 60 members. By the end of 1920, it had around 2000.

2) The German Workers' Party began to rely on him to get new party members, and in 1920 he was made chief of propaganda.

3) In 1920, the party was re-branded as the National Socialist German Workers' Party (the Nazi Party). In July 1921, Hitler became its leader.

4) The party was a nationalist party — it thought that the interests of Germans should be at the centre of government policy. It was anti-Semitic (anti-Jewish) and was opposed to the Weimar Republic. Above everything, it wanted to restore Germany's greatness.

5) This extract from one of Hitler's speeches shows his nationalist passion.

> 'For the murderers of our Fatherland who all the years through have betrayed and sold Germany, they are the same men who, as the November criminals, have plunged us into the depths of misfortune.
>
> We have the duty to speak since in the near future, when we have gained power, we shall have the further duty of taking [...] these traitors to their State and of hanging them on the gallows to which they belong.'
>
> *Extract from a speech made by Hitler in Munich in 1923.*

> Hitler implies Germany is a victim that has been 'betrayed'.

> He appears loyal to his country. He says it was Germany's 'duty' to get rid of 'traitors' like Weimar's 'November criminals'.

> Hitler wanted revenge. This appealed to many who felt Germany had been treated unfairly.

The Nazi Party Developed its Identity

As the Nazi Party grew in popularity, it established an identity that appealed to as many people as possible.

1) In February 1920, the Nazi Party promoted its policies in the 'Twenty-Five Point Programme'.

2) The Programme stressed the superiority of the German people and promoted anti-Semitism.

3) The party wanted to raise pensions, and improve health and education — but only for Germans.

4) Rejecting the Treaty of Versailles and promoting German greatness gave the party a nationwide appeal.

5) In 1921, Hitler founded his own party militia called the SA ('storm troopers'). The SA were political thugs — they carried out violent anti-Semitic attacks and intimidated rival political groups. Many people were scared of them, but some Germans admired them.

Extract from the Twenty-Five Point Programme:
- The Treaty of Versailles should be abolished.
- All German-speakers should be united.
- Only Germans (people with German blood) can be classed as citizens. Jews cannot be citizens.
- Improved pensions and land reform.

Comment and Analysis

The Nazis made Jewish people scapegoats for Germany's economic problems and encouraged Germans to blame them. The SA gave the party a military feel, which made it seem organised and disciplined. It also gave many ex-soldiers a job and a purpose.

Early Stages of the Nazi Party

Now you know all about the beginnings of the Nazi Party, but to get top marks in the exam, you need to use that knowledge to help you make connections and analyse sources.

Source Analysis

When you're making inferences from a source, you need to read between the lines. Think about the messages the author is trying to get across and how they want their audience to feel. This source comes from a speech that Hitler made in April 1922. He is explaining the Nazi Party's beliefs.

> At the founding of this Movement we… said to ourselves that to be 'national' means above everything to act with a boundless and all-embracing love for the people and, if necessary, even to die for it. And similarly to be 'social' means so to build up the State and the community of the people that every individual acts in the interest of the community of the people… And then we said to ourselves: there are no such things as classes: they cannot be… in Germany where everyone who is a German at all has the same blood, has the same eyes, and speaks the same language, here there can be no class, here there can be only a single people.

1) Copy and complete the table on the right, finding a detail from the source which demonstrates each Nazi belief.

2) What effect do you think the language used in this speech would have had on an audience? Give details from the source to support your answer.

Nazi belief	Evidence from speech
a) **Nationalist passion**	
b) **Restore German greatness**	
c) **Importance of German 'blood'**	
d) **Unite German speakers**	
e) **Support for German citizens**	

Thinking Historically

Here are five more points from the Nazi Party's Twenty-Five Point Programme:

- The government's most important duty should be caring for German citizens.
- The middle classes should be supported and protected.
- German territory should be expanded.
- The government should control all industries.
- All German citizens should have a job.

> Use your own knowledge, the extract from Hitler's speech above and the Twenty-Five Point Programme to answer Question 2.

1) What do you think the purpose of the Twenty-Five Point Programme was?
2) Make a list of the different groups in German society who might have found the Nazis appealing. Explain why the Nazis might have appealed to each group on your list.

Hitler was charismatic and stood for German greatness…

When you're dealing with a source, try to work out the basic details first, such as what it's about and who produced it. Then you can consider why it was made and what its message is.

The Munich Putsch

In 1922, a nationalist party <u>overthrew</u> the Italian government, inspiring Hitler to do the same in Germany.

Hitler tried to Overthrow the Government in the Munich Putsch

In 1923, the Weimar Republic was in <u>crisis</u>:

Hitler thought the time was right to attempt a putsch (revolt)...
- In 1923, things were going badly for the Weimar Republic — it seemed <u>weak</u>.
- <u>Hyperinflation</u> was at its peak and there were <u>food riots</u>.
- Many Germans were <u>angry</u> at the French and Belgian invasion of the <u>Ruhr</u> (see p.12). When the government <u>stopped resistance</u> by ending the strike there in 1923 (see p.14), discontent increased.

In November 1923, the Nazis marched on Munich...
- Hitler's soldiers occupied a <u>beer hall</u> in the Bavarian city of <u>Munich</u> where local government leaders were meeting. He announced that the <u>revolution</u> had begun.
- The next day Hitler marched into <u>Munich</u> supported by his stormtroopers. But news of the revolt had been <u>leaked</u> to the police, who were <u>waiting</u> for Hitler. The <u>police</u> fired on the rebels and the revolt quickly <u>collapsed</u>.

1) Hitler was <u>imprisoned</u> for his role in the Munich Putsch, but his trial gave him valuable <u>publicity</u>.

2) He wrote a book in prison called '<u>Mein Kampf</u>' ('My Struggle') describing his <u>beliefs</u> and <u>ambitions</u>.

3) Mein Kampf was vital in spreading Nazi <u>ideology</u> — millions of Germans read it. It introduced Hitler's belief that the Aryan race (which included Germans) was <u>superior</u> to all other races, and that all Germans had a right to '<u>Lebensraum</u>' (more space to live).

After the Munich Putsch Hitler Changed Tactics

1) By the <u>mid-1920s</u>, the German economy was starting to <u>recover</u> under <u>Stresemann</u> (see p.14). As a result, general support for the Nazis <u>declined</u> and overturning the government through a coup <u>no longer</u> seemed <u>realistic</u>.

2) The Nazi Party was <u>banned</u> after the Munich Putsch, along with the SA. Hitler was released from prison in December 1924 and the ban on the party was <u>lifted</u> in February 1925. Hitler <u>re-established</u> the Nazi Party with himself as <u>supreme leader</u>.

3) Hitler <u>changed tactics</u> — he now tried to gain control through the <u>democratic</u> system. This involved <u>restructuring</u> the Nazi Party so it could compete more successfully in <u>national</u> elections.

Comment and Analysis

The <u>dip</u> in support for the Nazi Party between 1924 and 1928 shows how important <u>economic unrest</u> was to Hitler's success. Nazi ideology <u>thrived</u> when Germany was <u>struggling</u>.

1 In 1926, Hitler held a conference with the Nazi leadership at <u>Bamberg</u>. He was worried that the party had become <u>divided</u> — some members wanted the party to go in a more <u>socialist</u> direction. He made it clear that the party would only follow <u>his</u> agenda.

3 Nazi propaganda increased and was <u>centrally controlled</u> by the leadership in Munich. This made propaganda campaigns more <u>efficient</u>. In 1926 Hitler re-established the <u>SA</u> and began to use them for propaganda purposes.

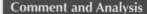

2 The Nazi Party adopted a <u>national</u> framework and became more <u>centralised</u>. In 1926 Hitler appointed leaders called '<u>gauleiters</u>' to run <u>regional</u> branches of the Nazi Party. Gauleiters were <u>controlled</u> by the party leadership in Munich, and supervised <u>district</u> and <u>local</u> branches of the party. This brought <u>every level</u> of the party under Hitler's control.

4 The Nazi Party created <u>new organisations</u> for different social groups. In 1926 it founded the <u>Hitler Youth</u> to attract younger voters, and it also created societies for different <u>professions</u>, e.g. The National Socialist Teachers' League. These organisations made different sectors of society feel <u>valued</u> by the party.

The Munich Putsch

As well as getting to grips with the dates and details of historical events, it's important that you're able to discuss their impact and significance. The activities below will help you to practise those skills.

Interpretation

Interpretation 1

The failure of the Munich Putsch made some nationalist groups lose faith in Hitler. They no longer believed that he was a capable political figure who could be trusted to attract and secure support. In their eyes, this poorly executed attempt to overthrow the government had finished Hitler's political career before it even began.

An extract from a textbook about Nazi Germany, written in 2018.

Interpretation 2

But the putsch, though a disastrous failure, had not done any harm to his personal prestige in rightist circles. On the contrary... the trial for high treason... provided [Hitler] with a first-class propaganda platform of which he made effective use; and his period of arrest... conferred on him a martyr's* halo.

An extract from a book by Eberhard Kolb, published in 1984.

*someone who is admired for suffering for their beliefs

1) Copy out the table below, summarising each interpretation's main argument about the consequences of the Putsch. Give evidence which could be used to support each argument. Use details from the interpretations and your own knowledge.

Interpretation	Main argument	Evidence
Interpretation 1		
Interpretation 2		

2) Using your completed table to help you, explain which interpretation you find most convincing about the consequences of the Putsch. Make sure you use evidence to support your argument.

Thinking Historically

In the years following the Munich Putsch, Hitler restructured the Nazi Party. He made four key changes to help the party become democratically elected.

1) What were the four changes Hitler made to the Nazi Party?
2) Explain why each change was important for the Nazi Party's success.

The Nazis needed to putsch a bit harder...

When you're giving your opinion on an interpretation, it's really important that you use your own knowledge of the topic to back up your view — always give as much detail as you can.

The Great Depression

The Wall Street Crash in 1929 caused the <u>Great Depression</u>, leading to a fall in <u>support</u> for the government.

The Wall Street Crash Ended economic Recovery

In October 1929 the Wall Street stock market in America <u>crashed</u>. It sparked an international economic <u>crisis</u> and meant the USA couldn't afford to <u>prop up</u> the German economy any longer.

1) Germany's economic recovery between 1924 and 1929 was built on <u>unstable</u> foundations. The biggest problem was that it was <u>dependent</u> on loans from the <u>USA</u>, which had been agreed in the Dawes Plan (see p.14).

2) After the Wall Street Crash, the USA <u>couldn't afford</u> to lend Germany money anymore. It <u>suspended</u> future payments and wanted some old loans to be repaid.

- Germany's economy <u>collapsed</u> without American aid. Industrial production went into <u>decline</u> — factories closed and banks went out of business.
- There was <u>mass unemployment</u>. In October 1929 <u>1.6 million</u> people were out of work, and by February 1932 there were over <u>6 million</u>.

Brüning's policies Decreased Support for Weimar

In March 1930, the Weimar Republic appointed a new Chancellor, <u>Heinrich Brüning</u>, to deal with the crisis. He introduced <u>tough</u> economic policies to keep inflation from rising like it had done in 1923 (see p.12).

Brüning's economic policies weren't popular...
- Brüning increased the cost of <u>imported</u> food to <u>help</u> German agriculture, but this also <u>raised</u> food prices.
- Government salaries and pensions were <u>reduced</u> and taxes <u>increased</u>.
- Social services were <u>cut back</u>, and <u>unemployment</u> benefits were reduced.

> As many Germans were <u>struggling</u> financially, the government seemed to be <u>adding</u> pressure by reducing support.

1) Everyday life in Germany seemed to be made <u>worse</u> by Brüning's policies.

2) They were designed to help the economy, but they also caused standards of living to <u>fall</u> — Brüning was nicknamed the 'Hunger Chancellor'.

3) By 1932, many different sectors of society were <u>discontent</u> with the Weimar government. High unemployment and reduced benefits also meant the government <u>lost</u> some backing from the working classes, who had always formed a <u>large part</u> of their support.

Comment and Analysis

<u>Not all</u> historians think that Brüning's policies made German society worse — some think the economic crisis was so <u>severe</u> that it would've taken <u>years</u> for any improvements to be seen.

The Government became Less Democratic

1) <u>Brüning's</u> economic policies were so <u>unpopular</u> that he had difficulty <u>passing</u> them in the Reichstag. He began to rely on '<u>Article 48</u>' of the Weimar constitution (see p.8). Brüning asked President Hindenburg to suspend the constitution, so he could make decisions <u>without</u> parliamentary approval.

2) By 1932, Brüning was regularly bypassing parliament to <u>force</u> his economic measures through.

Comment and Analysis

Weimar no longer felt like a <u>democracy</u> and the German people felt <u>neglected</u>. They began to look towards alternative political parties like the <u>Nazi Party</u> and the <u>Communist Party</u>.

The Great Depression

The Wall Street Crash caused an economic crisis which the Weimar government struggled to tackle. The activities on this page will help you to understand the key events and their wider impact.

Thinking Historically

The Wall Street Crash had a huge impact on German society, and contributed to the unpopularity of the Weimar Republic. The flowchart below shows how the Crash affected Germany.

1) Copy and complete the flowchart, listing the consequences of each event. Try to include as much detail as possible.

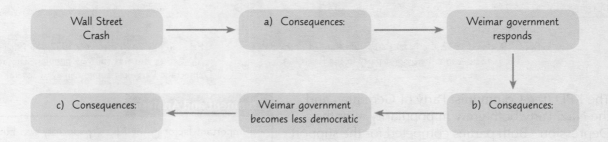

Wall Street Crash → a) Consequences: → Weimar government responds ↓

c) Consequences: ← Weimar government becomes less democratic ← b) Consequences:

2) Colour code your flowchart to show whether each development was an economic, political or social consequence of the Wall Street Crash.

3) Do you think the economic, social or political consequences of the Wall Street Crash were most significant for Germany? Explain your answer.

Source Analysis

This image shows a poster distributed by the Nazi Party before the presidential election in April 1932.

The text on the poster can be translated as 'Work! Freedom! Bread! Vote for the Nazi Party'.

1) Imagine you're using this source for an investigation into the impact of the Depression on German politics. Why is the date of this source significant?

2) This source is a piece of propaganda. Explain how this might affect the usefulness of the source for an investigation into the appeal of the Nazi Party in the early 1930s.

3) Why do you think the artist chose to include the words 'work', 'freedom' and 'bread' on the poster?

Germany's extremist parties became more attractive...

Thinking about why the creator of a source included particular details can really help you to understand the message the source is trying to get across and the audience it was aimed at.

Hitler's Rise to Power, 1919-33

The Rise of the Nazis

The <u>desperation</u> caused by the economic <u>Depression</u> in Germany in the 1920s and 1930s meant that the German people were willing to consider any political party that <u>promised</u> something <u>different</u>.

The Nazis increased in Popularity during the Depression

Popular discontent with the Weimar <u>government</u> and economic <u>instability</u> meant that many Germans had lost faith in democracy. This created an <u>opportunity</u> for extremist parties to grow.

Federal Election Results in Germany, 1928-32

1928	1930	July 1932	Nov 1932
Nazi Party: 3% Communist Party: 11% SPD 30%	Nazi Party: 18% Communist Party: 13% SPD 25%	Nazi Party: 37% Communist Party: 15% SPD 22%	Nazi Party: 33% Communist Party: 17% SPD 20%

Between 1928 and 1932, the Nazi Party <u>pulled ahead</u> of the KPD. The Nazis became the <u>biggest</u> party in the Reichstag.

Between July and November 1932, the Nazi Party <u>lost votes</u>, but was still very <u>popular</u>. The Social Democratic Party lost support in <u>every</u> federal election.

1) The KPD (the Communist Party of Germany) and the Nazi Party both grew in popularity after the Depression. Both parties <u>competed</u> for the <u>support</u> of Germans hit <u>hard</u> by the economic crisis.

2) Between 1928 and 1932, membership of the KPD grew from <u>130,000</u> to almost <u>300,000</u>. However, Nazi Party membership grew <u>even more</u> rapidly — soon the KPD got left behind.

Comment and Analysis

An important factor in the Nazis' popularity was Hitler's personality. Hitler was <u>patriotic</u> and <u>energetic</u>, and was able to effectively <u>convey</u> his enthusiasm to his supporters. His speeches brought <u>hope</u> to those who listened. In the Nazis' 1932 election campaigns, Hitler was depicted as Germany's <u>saviour</u> — he <u>stood up</u> to the Weimar government and <u>opposed</u> the 'threat' of communism.

The Nazi Party Appealed to many Different Groups in Society

The Nazis promised a more prosperous and less humiliating future, which was <u>very popular</u> among the German people — by <u>1930</u>, membership had grown to over <u>300,000</u>.

1) After the onset of the Depression, the Nazi Party's popularity <u>soared</u>. Hitler's promise to make Germany <u>great</u> again appealed to the growing ranks of <u>unemployed</u> and <u>young people</u> who wanted a <u>brighter future</u>.

2) Some people also supported the Nazis' <u>anti-communist</u> and <u>anti-Jewish</u> views. They saw communists and Jews as <u>scapegoats</u>, blaming them for Germany's <u>economic problems</u>.

3) Some wealthy <u>businessmen</u> who had lost out in the Great Depression turned to the Nazi Party. They <u>approved</u> of the Nazis' <u>anti-communist</u> stance and wanted the economic <u>prosperity</u> Hitler had promised.

Comment and Analysis

After the Depression hit Germany, more Germans began to <u>vote</u>. Participation in elections increased by around <u>10%</u> between 1928 and 1932. Many of these new voters were attracted by the <u>changes</u> the Nazi Party promised.

The Nazi Party was well organised...

*   By the 1930s, the Nazi Party seemed <u>strong</u> and <u>organised</u> in comparison to the Weimar government. The SA held demonstrations, distributed propaganda and appeared more <u>disciplined</u> than they had been in the early 1920s. The Nazi Party became more <u>respectable</u> and this helped Hitler secure support from the <u>middle classes</u>.
*   Propaganda was very <u>efficient</u>. It often focused on regional issues and targeted <u>specific groups</u>. This made individuals feel <u>valued</u> by the Party and stole votes from <u>smaller parties</u>.

The Rise of the Nazis

There's lots of tricky information to learn in this topic, but having a good grasp of the political scene will help you in the exam. Have a go at these activities to make sure you understand why Nazi support grew.

Knowledge and Understanding

The graph below shows the results of the four German federal elections that were held between 1928 and November 1932.

1) Using the information on page 28 to help you, label each line on the graph with the name of the party it represents.

2) Summarise how support for each party changed between 1928 and November 1932.

3) Why did extremist parties become more popular with voters in Depression-era Germany?

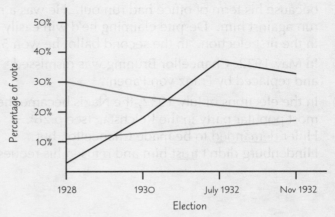

Source Analysis

This image is a Nazi election poster from 1932. It shows a crowd made up of people from different groups in society. The text on the poster can be translated as 'Our last hope: Hitler'.

1) Why do you think the Nazis included people from many different social groups in this election poster?

2) What impression does the poster create of life in the Weimar Republic? Support your answer with details from the source.

3) Why do you think the Nazis wanted to create this impression of life in the Weimar Republic?

4) What can you infer from the poster about why the Nazis were popular with voters in 1932?

The Nazis and Communists both gained in popularity...

It's important that you understand the pattern of election results for all the key parties in Depression-era Germany — you need to know more than just how the Nazi Party performed.

Hitler Becomes Chancellor

As the Depression got worse, <u>political instability</u> grew. Several parties were <u>competing</u> for power in the elections of 1932 (see p.28). In 1933, the Nazis would emerge <u>on top</u>. Hitler's rise continued.

Hindenburg Refused to give the Nazis power

1) By April 1932, economic conditions had <u>worsened</u>. The country was <u>desperate</u> for a <u>strong</u> government.

2) In the April 1932 presidential elections, President Hindenburg had to stand for <u>re-election</u> because his term of office had run out. He was a national hero, but Hitler decided to run against him. Despite claiming he'd win easily, Hindenburg <u>didn't</u> win a <u>majority</u> in the first election. In the second ballot he won 53%, beating Hitler's 36.8%.

3) In May 1932, Chancellor Brüning was dismissed and replaced by Franz von Papen.

4) In the elections of July 1932, the Nazis became the most <u>popular</u> party in the Reichstag (see p.28). Hitler <u>demanded</u> to be made Chancellor, but Hindenburg didn't <u>trust</u> him and <u>refused</u> his request.

> This could have been a <u>dead end</u> for Hitler — Hindenburg was the <u>only</u> one who could <u>legally</u> appoint him Chancellor of Germany.

Hitler became Chancellor with the aid of a Political Deal

1) The Nazis <u>lost</u> 34 seats in the November 1932 election — they seemed to be <u>losing</u> popularity.

2) In December 1932 Hindenburg replaced Papen with one of his advisors, <u>Kurt von Schleicher</u>. Schleicher tried to <u>cause divisions</u> in the Nazi Party by asking another leading Nazi to be Vice-Chancellor — Gregor Strasser. But Hitler <u>stopped</u> Strasser accepting.

3) Papen <u>resented</u> Schleicher because he suspected Schleicher had persuaded Hindenburg to dismiss him. He wanted to get back into government, so he made a <u>deal</u> with Hitler. They agreed that if Papen persuaded Hindenburg to make Hitler <u>Chancellor</u>, Hitler would make Papen <u>Vice-Chancellor</u>.

4) In January 1933, Papen persuaded Hindenburg to <u>replace</u> Schleicher with Hitler — Papen argued that they could <u>control Hitler</u> and use him as a puppet. He was <u>wrong</u>.

> 'In two months time we will have pushed Hitler so far into a corner, he'll be squeaking.' — Franz von Papen, 1933.

January 1932			July 1932		January 1933
There are <u>6 million</u> unemployed.	Hitler uses the <u>Depression</u> to promise <u>better things</u>.	Hitler stands against <u>Hindenburg</u> in 1932 and <u>loses</u>.	July 1932 — the Nazis are the <u>largest</u> party in the Reichstag with 230 seats.	The Nazis <u>lose</u> seats in November 1932 but are still the <u>largest</u> party.	Hitler is finally offered the <u>Chancellorship</u> in January 1933.

Here are two different <u>interpretations</u> of Hitler's rise to power. There's evidence to support <u>both</u> opinions.

Interpretation 1: 'After the onset of the Great Depression, Germans were willing to support <u>any</u> strong extremist party as an <u>alternative</u> to the democratic <u>Weimar government</u>.'

> <u>After</u> the Great Depression, <u>both</u> the Nazi Party <u>and</u> the Communist Party became more popular, and support for moderate parties like Social Democratic Party <u>dropped off</u>.

Interpretation 2: 'There was only one <u>credible</u> party to turn to after the Great Depression hit — the Nazi Party. It was the only party with a <u>charismatic leader</u> who had <u>mass appeal</u>.'

> The Nazi Party grew <u>more rapidly</u> than any other party after 1928. Hitler's passion and energy made the Nazis <u>stand out</u>, and support for the KPD simply <u>couldn't</u> keep up.

Hitler Becomes Chancellor

There are many reasons why Hitler became Chancellor. This page will help you break it all down.

Knowledge and Understanding

1) Copy out the timeline below and add the events that took place in each of the months given.

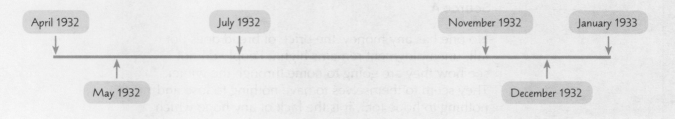

Interpretation

Interpretation 1

Hindenburg had begun to dig Weimar's grave by hollowing out parliamentary democracy in the era of the presidential cabinets*. Yet he... had not been ready to appoint the Nazi leader as Chancellor [in 1932]. When that changed in January 1933, Hindenburg became an undertaker of the Republic for whose salvation many on the left and the centre had re-elected him less than a year before.

An extract written by Anna von der Goltz and published in 2009.

*the period from 1930 to 1933 when governments were formed by the President instead of by Parliament

Interpretation 2

If one can conceive of the twentieth century without the Great Depression — very difficult, to be sure, but worth the exercise — then it is possible to imagine the [Weimar] republic gradually winning to its side majority support. In 1928, prior to the onset of the Depression, the Nazis were a marginal political force, reaping only 2.6 per cent in the national election that year. They were still banned in many states and... a move back toward the centre, toward the Weimar Coalition parties... is evident in the statistics. The republic could have survived, but not amid a Depression that left one-third of the workforce unemployed.

An extract written by Eric D. Weitz and published in 2018.

1) What does each interpretation argue was the most important factor in the fall of the Weimar Republic? Give a detail from each interpretation to support your answer.

2) How do the sources on pages 27 and 29 support the main argument in Interpretation 2?

3) For each interpretation, make a mind map of evidence which could be used to support its main argument. Use evidence from the interpretation and information from pages 26-30 to help you.

Papen and Hindenburg misjudged Hitler's strength...

EXAM TIP *You need to know Hitler's rise to power in full for the exam. Make sure you know the order in which events happened, the names of all the key figures and the roles these figures played.*

Worked Exam-Style Question

Have a look at the sample answer below, which shows you how to draw inferences from a source. There may be several things you can infer from the source, but you only need to discuss two points in this question.

Source A

No one has any money, the price of bread does not fall, unemployment remains high... People do not see how they are going to come through the winter. They seem to themselves to have nothing to lose and nothing to hope for... it is the lack of any hope which makes the situation seem to them so depressing and makes it difficult for Brüning to keep them in hand.

*A description of living conditions in Germany
sent by British diplomat Sir Horace Rumbold
to the Foreign Office on 29 May 1931.*

Extract abridged by Julia Boyd

Infer two things from Source A about the impact of the Great Depression in Germany. Explain each inference that you make. [4 marks]

> I can infer from the source that during the Great Depression many Germans struggled to survive. The author emphasises that people couldn't afford food because they had no money and the price of bread stayed high — they didn't know 'how they [were] going to come through the winter'. This suggests that living conditions were extremely poor.
> I can also infer from the source that the Great Depression led to political instability in Germany. Rumbold states that Chancellor Brüning found it difficult to keep people 'in hand' because they had 'nothing to hope for'. This suggests that Brüning's failure to resolve economic problems and improve people's living conditions caused unrest.

State clearly what you can <u>infer</u> from the source — i.e. what the source <u>tells you</u> about the impact of the Great Depression.

Remember to list <u>two things</u> you can infer, but no more.

Explain <u>which details</u> in the source support your inference.

Exam-Style Questions

Try these exam-style questions on the reasons behind Hitler's success and the end of the Weimar Republic.

Interpretation 1

An extract from a study of Hitler by Ian Kershaw, published in 1987.

> In such conditions as prevailed* in the last phase of the Weimar Republic...
> Salvation could only be sought with a leader who possessed *personal* power
> and was prepared to take *personal* responsibility, sweeping away the causes of
> the misery and faceless politicians and bureaucrats** who prevail over it, and
> seeming to impose his own personal power upon the force of history itself.

*were widespread   **government officials

Interpretation 2

An extract from a book about the rise of the Nazi Party by Julia Boyd, published in 2017.

> [According to Christopher Isherwood*, after the Wall Street Crash]
> 'The Berlin brew seethed with unemployment, malnutrition, stock
> market panic, hatred of the Versailles treaty and other potent ingredients.'
> In other words, exactly the conditions required by the National Socialists
> to convince voters that Hitler's own brew of dictatorship, hatred and
> perverted patriotism** offered their only hope of national renewal.

*a novelist from England who lived in Berlin in the early 1930s   **love for your country

Exam-Style Questions

1) Explain why the Great Depression weakened support for the Weimar Republic.
   You could mention unemployment and Chancellor Brüning in your answer,
   but you should also use your own knowledge.   [12 marks]

2) Look at Interpretations 1 and 2, which give different opinions about
   the reasons behind the growing popularity of the Nazi Party after 1929.
   Explain the main difference between the two opinions.   [4 marks]

3) Give one reason why Interpretations 1 and 2 might express different opinions
   about the reasons behind the growing popularity of the Nazi Party after 1929.   [4 marks]

4) To what extent do you agree with the opinion expressed
   in Interpretation 2 about the reasons behind the growing
   popularity of the Nazi Party after 1929? You should refer
   to both interpretations and use your own knowledge to
   support your answer.   [16 marks]

> For questions like this in
> the exam, 4 extra marks
> will be awarded for spelling,
> punctuation, grammar and
> using specialist terminology.

Achieving Total Power

After Hitler became <u>Chancellor</u> in January 1933, he took measures to establish a <u>dictatorship</u>.

The Nazis used Dirty Tricks to Win in 1933

Hitler needed to <u>increase</u> the Nazi Party's seats in the Reichstag to get a majority and be able to pass <u>new laws</u>. If they got a two-thirds majority, then the Nazi Party would be able to make <u>changes</u> to the <u>constitution</u>.

1) In the elections of March 1933, the Nazis took <u>no chances</u>. Hitler tried to <u>stop</u> other political parties from carrying out <u>effective</u> campaigns. They <u>controlled</u> the news media, and opposition meetings were <u>banned</u>.

2) Hitler used the SA (see p.22) to <u>terrorise</u> opponents. In February 1933, the SA raided the Communist Party <u>headquarters</u> in Berlin and claimed to have found evidence that the communists were planning an <u>uprising</u> against the government.

3) In February 1933, just 6 days before the elections, a <u>fire</u> broke out in the Reichstag. Hitler blamed the <u>Communist Party</u> and used the event to whip up <u>anti-communist</u> feelings.

> This would mean the Nazi Party could <u>change</u> the way the government was <u>structured</u> and give Hitler <u>absolute power</u>.

- Hitler used the fire to claim that communists were a <u>threat</u> to the country. Nazi newspapers used the event as an excuse to publish anti-communist <u>conspiracy</u> theories.
- President Hindenburg <u>issued</u> a decree giving Hitler <u>emergency powers</u> to deal with the supposed communist <u>threat</u> — many basic rights given to the German people under the Weimar constitution, e.g. freedom of speech, were <u>suspended</u>.
- Hitler used these powers to <u>intimidate</u> communist voters. The decree also enabled the SA to <u>round up</u> and <u>imprison</u> nearly 4000 communist members.

Comment and Analysis

The emergency powers granted to Hitler were a <u>turning point</u> — they mark the first step towards making Germany a <u>dictatorship</u>. Hitler justified them by saying that they were necessary to protect the German people. This meant he faced <u>little opposition</u> from the German public.

The Enabling Act helped Hitler to create a Dictatorship

1) In the March 1933 elections, the Nazi Party won 288 seats but <u>didn't</u> have an overall majority. So Hitler simply made the <u>Communist Party</u> (which had 81 seats) <u>illegal</u>.

2) This gave him enough <u>support</u> in parliament to bring in the <u>Enabling Act</u>, passed with <u>threats</u> and <u>bargaining</u> in March 1933. This let him <u>govern</u> for four years <u>without</u> parliament.

3) The Enabling Act was an important step in Hitler's <u>consolidation</u> of power. It allowed Hitler to bring <u>controversial</u> legislation into force to <u>strengthen</u> the Nazi Party's position.

> Hitler could now pass laws and amend the constitution <u>without</u> the <u>Reichstag's</u> consent. Other Chancellors in the Weimar government had used <u>Article 48</u> to bypass parliament (see p.26), so the new Act may <u>not</u> have seemed that extreme to some Germans.

1 In May 1933, Hitler abolished Trade Unions and arrested union officials.

> Hitler saw Trade Unions as a <u>threat</u> because they had great <u>influence</u> over the working class. After May 1933, workers had to join the Nazi-controlled <u>Labour Front</u> instead.

2 In July 1933, all political parties, apart from the Nazi Party, were banned.

> The new law also banned <u>new</u> parties from forming. After July 1933, Germany was officially a <u>one-party state</u>.

Comment and Analysis

Some Germans thought a one-party state would be an <u>improvement</u>. Parties often couldn't reach an <u>agreement</u> in the Reichstag and Germans were tired of political <u>instability</u> — between March 1930 and March 1933, there were <u>four</u> different Chancellors.

Achieving Total Power

Have a go at the activities on this page to test your understanding of how the Nazis built a dictatorship.

Thinking Historically

In 1932, the communists were an important political party in Germany, but by the middle of 1933 they had been outlawed and Germany had become a one-party state.

1) Draw a flowchart to show how the communists lost power in 1933.

There's an example of a flowchart on page 27.

Interpretation

Interpretation 1

The Reichstag Fire was either a stroke of genius from the Nazis or a stroke of luck. By blaming the fire on the Communists, the Nazis gave themselves an excuse to discredit, intimidate and suppress some of their most influential opponents to an extent that had not previously been possible.

An extract from a history book about the rise of the Nazis, written in 2018.

Interpretation 2

It nevertheless took Hitler some time to extend his hold on power... Elections were called for 5 March 1933, and, despite the intimidating atmosphere following the burning of the Reichstag on 27 February, which the Nazis used as a pretext for declaring a state of emergency, the Nazis still failed to win an absolute majority at the polls.

An extract from a book by Mary Fulbrook, published in 1997.

In the exam, it's important to structure your essays clearly. In each paragraph, you should make a point, set out some relevant evidence from the interpretation or from your own knowledge and then explain why the evidence supports your opening point.

1) Interpretation 1 argues that the Reichstag fire was one of the most important stages in Hitler's consolidation of power. Use the table below to help you structure an essay explaining how far you agree with this view. Each row should represent a paragraph of your essay.

Point	Evidence	Why evidence supports point
The Reichstag fire was important because it allowed the Nazis to discredit their main opposition.	The Nazis blamed the communists for the fire and used it as an excuse to publish anti-communist conspiracy theories.	This helped Hitler to consolidate his power because it encouraged people to see the communists as a threat. By suggesting the communists were violent and dangerous, it also justified the Nazis' own use of violence.

Add three rows to the table to plan three more paragraphs.

Make sure you include arguments both for and against Interpretation 1.

You need to write about both interpretations to get top marks in the exam.

Democracy in Germany had gone up in flames...

In the exam, remember to consider people's circumstances and the limited knowledge they had at the time. Ordinary Germans had no idea what the Nazi Party would grow into after 1933.

Achieving Total Power

Hitler had power, but he still had enemies.

The SA was a Threat to Hitler

1) The SA (a 'private Nazi Party army' of over 400,000 men — see p.22) had helped Hitler come to power.

2) But Hitler now saw the SA as a threat, because its members were loyal to Ernst Röhm, the SA's leader.

3) The SA was also unpopular with the leaders of the German army and with some ordinary Germans.

The 'Night of the Long Knives' — Hitler removes his enemies

1) Ernst Röhm was the biggest threat to Hitler, but Hitler was also worried about other members of the Nazi Party who disagreed with his views.

2) On the 29th-30th June 1934, Hitler sent men to arrest or kill Röhm and others. Altogether, several hundred people were killed or imprisoned, including Röhm and various other leaders of the SA and senior politicians.

3) Hitler claimed that those who had been killed had been plotting to overthrow the government, so he declared their murders legal.

4) This became known as the 'Night of the Long Knives', and was a triumph for Hitler.

5) It stamped out all potential opposition within the Nazi party and sent a powerful message to the party about Hitler's ruthlessness and brutality. It also showed that Hitler was now free to act above the law.

> **Comment and Analysis**
>
> Most Germans wouldn't have known exactly what had happened on the 'Night of the Long Knives' until a few days later, when Hitler declared the events legal. Even then, there was little outcry. It's likely that some people believed Hitler's claims that the violence was necessary to protect the country. Others were too scared to speak out.

Hitler took full control of National and Local government

1) In August 1934, Hindenburg died. Hitler used the opportunity to combine the posts of Chancellor and President, and also made himself Commander-in-Chief of the army.

2) He called himself Der Führer (the leader) — this was the beginning of the dictatorship.

3) At this point, Hitler reorganised local government — in 1926 he had created branches of the Nazi Party in different areas of Germany called Gau (plural: Gaue). These now became official provinces of Germany, with a Gauleiter (a loyal Nazi) in charge of each (see p.24).

4) Above them were the Reichsleiters, who advised Hitler, e.g. Goebbels who was in charge of propaganda, and Himmler who was chief of the German police.

5) At the top and in absolute control was the Führer — Hitler.

6) Every aspect of life was carefully controlled, and only loyal Nazis could be successful.

The Führer
↓
Reichsleiters
↓
Gauleiters
↓
Other Officials

> Gauleiters were appointed by Hitler, which ensured he had control over the lower levels of the party.

> These included local and district party leaders.

> **Comment and Analysis**
>
> When the Nazis took over, some Germans were glad that someone was at last taking control after the chaos and political weaknesses of the Weimar years.

> The army had to swear an oath of allegiance to Hitler, instead of pledging to protect Germany. Some German workers were also forced to take an oath of obedience, promising loyalty to Hitler. Those who refused could lose their jobs.

Nazi Control and Dictatorship, 1933-39

Achieving Total Power

Within just a few years of becoming Chancellor, Hitler had managed to establish a dictatorship in Germany. The activities below will help you to explore some of the facts in more detail.

Interpretation

On page 35, you used a table to structure an essay explaining how far you agree with the view that the Reichstag fire was one of the most important stages in Hitler's consolidation of power.

1) Use the information on page 36 to add two new rows to your table.

Knowledge and Understanding

The diagram below shows the structure of local government in Nazi Germany.

1) Copy and complete the diagram, filling in the title of each official and adding as much extra information about them as you can.

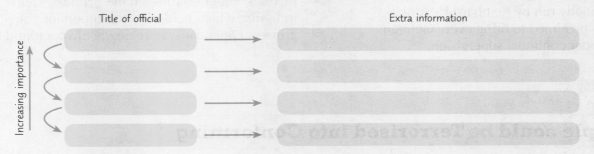

Title of official   Extra information

Increasing importance

2) Explain how Hitler's reorganisation of government helped him to achieve total power.

Source Analysis

The source below comes from a speech made by Hitler to the Reichstag on 13th July 1934. He is explaining why he ordered the 'Night of the Long Knives' on 29th-30th June 1934.

> The natural relationship between the Party and the SA slowly started to become weaker. We were able to detect what seemed like deliberate attempts to withdraw the SA more and more from the mission I had given them, in order to make them serve other tasks or interests.

1) Imagine you are using this source for an investigation into the reasons for the 'Night of the Long Knives'. Explain how each feature of the source listed below affects its usefulness for your investigation.

   a) Author   b) Date   c) Purpose   d) Content

The Nazis — eliminating opposition...

You'll be marked on your spelling, punctuation and grammar in question 3(d) in the exam, so try to leave a few minutes at the end to check over your work and correct any mistakes.

The Machinery of Terror

The Nazis aimed to make Germany a <u>totalitarian state</u> (where the government controls <u>all aspects</u> of life).

Germany became a Police State

1) The Nazis wanted <u>complete control</u> over the <u>machinery of government</u> and <u>people's lives</u>.

2) Hitler's Enabling Act of 1933 (see p.34) allowed the government to <u>read</u> people's mail, <u>listen in</u> on their phone calls, and <u>search</u> their homes without notice.

3) The <u>Law for the Reconstruction of the Reich</u> (1934) gave the Nazis total power over local governments.

4) There were <u>laws</u> to sack civil servants who didn't support the Nazis and accept their rules.

5) The Nazis also made changes to the <u>justice system</u>. <u>Judges</u> didn't have to be 'fair' and unbiased. Instead, they were expected to make rulings that were in line with <u>Nazi Party policy</u>.

6) The <u>Sicherheitsdienst</u> (SD) was the Nazi intelligence service. It was initially run by <u>Reinhard Heydrich</u> — he aimed to bring every German under continual supervision.

> **The legal system was far from fair...**
> - In 1933, the Nazis set up <u>special courts</u> where the basic rights of those accused were <u>suspended</u> — they couldn't <u>appeal</u> or <u>question</u> evidence given against them.
> - In 1934, Hitler established the <u>People's Court</u> in Berlin, which held trials for important <u>political</u> crimes. Defendants were nearly always found <u>guilty</u>.

People could be Terrorised into Conforming

The government was also prepared to use <u>terror</u> and even <u>violence</u> against the German people.

1) The <u>SS</u> (<u>Schutzstaffel</u>) began as a bodyguard for Hitler. It expanded massively under the leadership of Himmler during the 1930s. Its members were totally loyal to Hitler, and feared for their <u>cruelty</u>.

2) Himmler was also in charge of the <u>secret police</u> — the <u>Gestapo</u>. The Gestapo's job was 'to protect public safety and order', but their methods included harsh interrogations and imprisonment without trial.

3) Local <u>wardens</u> were employed to make sure Germans were loyal to the Nazis. Members of the public were encouraged to <u>report disloyalty</u>. Many were arrested by the Gestapo as a result.

4) After 1933, <u>concentration camps</u> were created across Germany and its territories to hold political prisoners and anybody else considered dangerous to the Nazis. Some of these were later turned into <u>death camps</u>.

Security Police search a car in Berlin on the orders of the Gestapo.

© Mary Evans / Sueddeutsche Zeitung Photo

Not everyone lived in Constant Terror

1) Most Germans were prepared to <u>go along with</u> the new regime. Some people accepted the new rules out of <u>fear</u>.

2) Others went along with them because they <u>believed in their aims</u>, even if they didn't approve of the Nazis' brutal methods.

> **Comment and Analysis**
>
> For those that <u>didn't fit in</u> with the Nazi ideals (e.g. Jews), life under the SS and the Gestapo could be terrifying. But Hitler was <u>supported</u>, <u>not feared</u>, by many Germans.

The Machinery of Terror

The nature of the police state in Nazi Germany has been debated by historians. Try the activities below.

Knowledge and Understanding

1) Copy and complete the mind map below, adding as many features of the Nazi police state as you can. Explain how each feature helped the Nazis to control people.

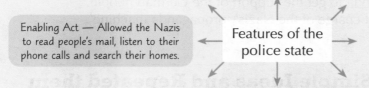

Enabling Act — Allowed the Nazis to read people's mail, listen to their phone calls and search their homes.

Features of the police state

Interpretation

Joll suggests that the police state was largely hidden, but still frightening for ordinary people.

Joll argues that the Nazi police state became more powerful and frightening over time.

Interpretation 1

<u>Behind</u> the new corporate* organisations, the control of education and of the media of communication, the official culture, the mass rallies and the mass movements, lay the <u>shadow</u> of the terror and the fear of the concentration camp. People disappeared and were never heard of again, <u>neighbours denounced** each other</u>; children informed on their parents. As time went on, and especially in the later years of the war, the <u>terror increased</u>, and the number of concentration camps... grew.

An extract from a book by James Joll, published in 1973.

According to the interpretation, ordinary people both participated in and were affected by the police state.

*united   **informed the authorities about

1) Summarise the main argument of Interpretation 1.

Interpretation 2

The population was more than merely implicated reluctantly in the use of terror: terror — or more precisely, specific manifestations of terror — met with <u>popular approval</u>... The terror, directed against political or social 'trouble-makers', was not only not concealed from the population... but was <u>highly visible</u>, was documented in the press during the Third Reich, was given legitimacy in the speeches of the Reich's leaders and was <u>approved and welcomed</u> by many Germans.

An extract from a book by Detlev J.K. Peukert, published in 1987.

2) Explain what each highlighted phrase in Interpretation 2 suggests about the Nazi police state. Use the example of Interpretation 1 above to help you.

3) How is the main argument of Interpretation 2 different from the main argument of Interpretation 1?

4) Why do you think the arguments in the two interpretations are different?

The Nazis exercised control using any means necessary...

In the exam, you'll be asked to explain one difference between the views in two interpretations. Make sure you focus on the most important difference — don't waste time writing about others.

Propaganda

The Nazis also used <u>propaganda</u> to help them control the German people's lives.

Propaganda aims to Control how people Think

1) Propaganda means spreading information that <u>influences</u> how people <u>think</u> and <u>behave</u>.

2) It gives only certain <u>points of view</u> and often <u>leaves out important facts</u>.

3) The <u>Nazis</u> used <u>powerful propaganda</u> to get the support of the German people. <u>Dr Joseph Goebbels</u> was in overall charge of the Nazis' 'propaganda machine'.

Nazi propaganda took Simple Ideas and Repeated them

1) Nazi propaganda was used to <u>unite</u> the German people and convince them that the Nazis would make Germany <u>strong</u>.

2) Germans were encouraged to <u>hate</u> the countries that signed the <u>Treaty of Versailles</u>. The Nazis said Germany should <u>fight</u> to get back the territory '<u>stolen</u>' by the treaty.

3) Goebbels created the '<u>Hitler Myth</u>', which made Hitler seem like a god and the saviour of Germany. This was the '<u>cult of the Führer</u>'.

4) The Nazis' propaganda also said that <u>Jews</u> and <u>communists</u> were the biggest cause of <u>Germany's problems</u>. One Nazi paper claimed that Jews <u>murdered children</u> for the Passover Feast.

> A popular slogan was '<u>One people, one empire, one leader</u>'. Many Germans <u>devoted their lives</u> to Hitler.

5) The Nazis encouraged a return to <u>traditional</u> German <u>values</u> and a revival of <u>traditional</u> German <u>culture</u>.

The Government had to Approve all Artistic Works

1) Goebbels founded the <u>Ministry of Public Enlightenment and Propaganda</u> in <u>1933</u>.

2) It had departments for <u>music</u>, <u>theatre</u>, <u>film</u>, <u>literature</u> and <u>radio</u>. All artists, writers, journalists and musicians had to <u>register</u> to get their <u>work approved</u>.

Nazis used the Media as a tool of Propaganda

1) The Nazis wanted to <u>surround</u> people with their propaganda. They used <u>censorship</u> to prevent Germans from seeing or hearing anything that gave a <u>different message</u>.

2) They sold <u>cheap radios</u> and <u>controlled broadcasts</u>. By 1939 approximately <u>70%</u> of households had a radio, which gave the Nazis a <u>voice</u> in most people's <u>homes</u>.

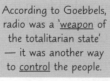

> According to Goebbels, radio was a '<u>weapon</u> of the totalitarian state' — it was another way to <u>control</u> the people.

3) In 1933, only 3% of German daily newspapers were controlled by the Nazis. By 1944, this had risen to <u>82%</u>. This meant the Nazis could decide what was published in the papers.

4) The Nazis also produced hundreds of <u>films</u>. Many films showed the <u>strengths</u> of the Nazis and Hitler, and the weakness of their opponents. An important German director was <u>Leni Riefenstahl</u>.

5) Another method of spreading propaganda was through <u>posters</u> showing the evil of Germany's enemies and the power of Hitler. Propaganda also let Germans know what was <u>expected</u> of them.

Nazi propaganda poster, 1935. It says that 'the German student' fights for the Führer and for the German people.

Propaganda

Propaganda was an effective tool for the Nazis. This page will help you break down how it worked.

Source Analysis

The source on the right is a Nazi propaganda poster made in the 1930s. The text reads 'Long Live Germany!'

© Prisma by Dukas Presseagentur GmbH / Alamy Stock Photo

1) Copy and complete the diagram below by adding as many details from the poster as possible. You can use each detail more than once.

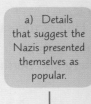

a) Details that suggest the Nazis presented themselves as popular.

b) Details that suggest the Nazis presented themselves as Germany's saviours.

c) Details that suggest the Nazis presented Hitler as a great leader.

2) In the boxes below, there are three possible investigations about Nazi propaganda. Which investigation do you think this source would be most useful for? Explain your choice.

a) How effective was Hitler's leadership?

b) What were the messages of Nazi propaganda?

c) How successfully did Nazi propaganda change people's attitudes?

3) Why do you think the source would be less useful for the other two investigations?

Knowledge and Understanding

1) Explain who Joseph Goebbels was and what his role was within the Nazi Party.
2) Write a brief definition for each of the following terms:
   a) Propaganda
   b) Censorship
3) Summarise the five main messages of Nazi propaganda.
4) Copy and complete the table below, listing the different propaganda techniques used by the Nazis and explaining how each one was used. Add as many rows as you need.

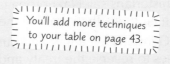
You'll add more techniques to your table on page 43.

Technique	How the Nazis used it

EXAM TIP

Radio Nazi — broadcasting to you wherever you are...

Remember that just because a source is a piece of propaganda, it doesn't mean that it's useless to historians. A propaganda poster can tell us lots about the image the Nazis wanted to create.

Nazi Control and Dictatorship, 1933-39

Propaganda

Nazi propaganda was <u>sophisticated</u> and it was <u>everywhere</u>.

Nazi propaganda could involve Spectacular Displays

1) The Nazis used <u>public rallies</u> to spread their propaganda. The annual <u>Nuremberg Rallies</u> focused on speeches by leading Nazis, like Hitler and Goebbels. The 1934 Nuremberg Rally was recorded by Riefenstahl in her film '<u>Triumph of the Will</u>'.

Hermann Goering at a Nuremberg Rally, as shown in 'Triumph of the Will'.

2) One million people attended the 1936 rally. There were displays of <u>lights</u> and <u>flags</u> to greet the arrival of Hitler. These made him look <u>more powerful</u>.

3) Sporting events like the <u>1936 Berlin Olympics</u> were used to show off German wealth and power. But the success of non-Aryan athletes like African-American <u>Jesse Owens</u> (who won four gold medals) undermined Hitler's message.

4) Nazi power was also shown through <u>art</u> and <u>architecture</u>, and grand new buildings appeared in Nuremberg and Berlin.

Propaganda was used to change Culture and Society

1) The Nazis promised an empire that would last a <u>thousand years</u> — based on <u>traditional values</u>.

2) <u>Modern art</u> was banned, in favour of realistic paintings that fit with Nazi ideology. Modern art was labelled '<u>degenerate</u>' and exhibitions were created to show people how 'bad' it was. The Nazis celebrated the works of '<u>German</u>' composers, such as Wagner, but much <u>modern classical music</u>, works by <u>Jewish composers</u>, and <u>jazz</u> were all attacked.

3) <u>School textbooks</u> were rewritten to make Germans look successful. Children were taught to believe in <u>Nazi doctrines</u> (see p.52).

4) The '<u>Strength through Joy</u>' programme sought to show ordinary workers that the Nazi regime cared about their standard of living (see p.50).

> In the <u>Weimar Republic</u>, artists had started to use ideas that were <u>new</u> and <u>experimental</u>. For more about this, see p.16.

Propaganda was most Effective when Reinforcing Existing Ideas

Surprisingly, it's quite <u>difficult</u> to tell how <u>effective</u> Nazi propaganda was.

1) Some historians say Nazi propaganda was better at <u>reinforcing</u> people's <u>existing attitudes</u> than making them believe <u>something different</u>.

2) Many Germans felt angry and humiliated by the <u>Treaty of Versailles</u>, so Hitler's promises to reverse the treaty and make Germany great again were very <u>popular</u>.

3) After the <u>political weakness</u> of the Weimar Republic, people found the image of Hitler as a <u>strong</u> leader appealing. So the '<u>Hitler Myth</u>' was very effective and made Hitler an extremely <u>popular</u> leader.

4) <u>Anti-Jewish</u> and <u>anti-communist</u> attitudes already existed in Germany <u>before</u> the Nazis came to power.

5) The <u>Weimar Republic</u> was seen as too <u>liberal</u> by many — they thought standards in Germany had slipped. These people liked the promise of a return to <u>traditional</u> German values.

6) The Depression had left many German people in <u>poverty</u>. This made them easier to <u>persuade</u>, and the Nazis' promises of help extremely <u>popular</u>.

> **Comment and Analysis**
>
> However effective their propaganda was, the Nazis' <u>control</u> of the media made it almost <u>impossible</u> for anyone to publish an <u>alternative</u> point of view.

Propaganda

Here's a whole new page of exercises about propaganda for you to have a go at.

Thinking Historically

1) On page 41, you made a table of some Nazi propaganda techniques.
Complete your table by adding all the propaganda techniques covered on page 42.

2) Look back at your summary of the main messages of Nazi propaganda from page 41. Using page 42 to help you, explain why each message might have appealed to people in Germany.

Source Analysis

Source 1

There is a particular quality about Nazi propaganda; it is not believed, yet it works. The close collaboration of Dr Goebbels with the lie is just as widely known inside Germany as outside. Only the most stupid accept word for word the claims and pretensions of the Ministry of Propaganda. But even the cleverest are affected by it, as they are by commercial posters.

An extract from a book by a German journalist called Sebastian Haffner. It was published in 1940, two years after Haffner emigrated from Germany to Britain with his Jewish fiancée.

Source 2

No other political movement has understood the art of propaganda as well as the National Socialists... What distinguishes it from all other political parties is the ability to see into the soul of the people and to speak the language of the man on the street.

An extract from a text about Nazi propaganda written by Joseph Goebbels in 1931.

1) Copy and complete the table below by explaining how the authorship and date of Source 1 influence its usefulness for an investigation into the effectiveness of Nazi propaganda in the 1930s.

Feature	Usefulness
a) Content	The source is useful because it refers directly to the issue of how and why Nazi propaganda worked. Its usefulness is limited because it refers to propaganda generally, without explaining how different people were affected by different kinds of propaganda.
b) Author	
c) Date	

2) Make another copy of the table above. Fill it in by explaining how the content, authorship and date of Source 2 affect its usefulness for an investigation into the effectiveness of Nazi propaganda in the 1930s.

Nazi spin — sophisticated, but probably not 100% effective...

You'll have to write about two different sources for question 3(a) in the exam, but you don't need to compare them. Just take each source in turn and explain how useful it is.

Worked Exam-Style Question

This sample answer will help you to explain the usefulness of some sources.

Source A

© Mary Evans Picture Library/WEIMAR ARCHIVE

A German girl decorates a picture of Adolf Hitler with flowers. Photograph taken in Germany in 1935.

Source B

The German peasant has become impoverished... the social hopes of many millions of people are destroyed; one third of all German men and women of working age is unemployed... If the present parties seriously want to save Germany, why have they not done so already? Had they wanted to save Germany, why has it not happened?

Extract from a public speech made by Adolf Hitler in July, 1932.

Explain how useful Sources A and B are for an investigation into what the Nazi Party offered the German people. Use both sources, as well as your own knowledge. [8 marks]

> Make it clear which source you're talking about.

> Ask yourself about the source — who made it, when they made it, where and for what purpose.

Source A is partially useful because it shows that the Nazi Party was offering the German people a strong leader who was admired and loved by his people. The photo was taken by an unknown photographer in 1935 — two years into Hitler's Chancellorship, when he was consolidating his dictatorship. By 1935, the Nazi Party had established a system of censorship to control the image of the party, so it is possible that this photograph was taken as a propaganda image, which limits its usefulness because propaganda aims to portray a certain message. The photo's suggestion that the Nazi Party offered a strong and loved leader isn't necessarily false — Hitler's charisma and patriotism were undoubtedly a factor in the Nazi Party's popularity. However, it's unlikely that photos published at that time would challenge Nazi Party ideology, making Source A unreliable in showing what German people felt the Nazi Party offered them. Because of this, Source A is only partially useful.

> Remember to say how useful you think each source is.

> Remember to write about both sources.

Source B is from a speech made by Hitler himself in July 1932. The fact that the speech was made by the leader of the Nazi Party is useful because it shows what Hitler was directly offering the people of Germany. Hitler talks about the need to 'save Germany', which suggests that the Nazi Party wanted to be seen by the German people as offering hope. In mid-1932, the Nazi Party was trying to appeal to as many people as possible before elections in November. This view is from the Nazi Party's perspective, and as a result it is only partially useful. Both sources focus on the impression the Party was trying to give — not on what Germans themselves believed. This means that both sources are only partially useful at best.

> Use evidence from the source to support the points that you've made.

> Think about when the sources were created, and how that affects their usefulness.

> You can also write about what the sources don't include.

Nazi Control and Dictatorship, 1933-39

Exam-Style Questions

Source A

An extract from an interview with a woman who lived in Nazi Germany.
The interview took place around 50 years after the end of the Second World War.

> For many years... we were kept under surveillance. Someone from
> the police would come by, albeit in civilian clothes, and make
> inquiries to see if we were doing things like greeting one another
> with "Heil Hitler." They even went to our landlord, who owned the
> building, and asked her, "What kind of impression do you have?"

Source B

A cartoon produced in Nazi Germany by German artist A. Paul Weber.
Weber was involved in resistance against the Nazis in the 1930s. The
cartoon is called 'The Snooper' and shows someone spying on a neighbour.

Exam-Style Questions

1) Infer two things from Source A about the nature of the
   Nazi police state. Explain each inference that you make.   [4 marks]

2) Explain how useful Sources A and B are for an investigation into
   how the Nazis controlled the German population. Use both
   sources, as well as your own knowledge, to support your answer.   [8 marks]

3) Explain why Nazi propaganda was effective. You could
   mention censorship and traditional values in your
   answer, but you should also use your own knowledge.   [12 marks]

Attitudes Towards the Church

The Nazi Party publicly supported religious freedom, but in reality saw Christianity as a threat.

Hitler wanted to Reduce the Church's Power

1) In the 1930s, most Germans were Christians and the Church was very influential. During the Weimar Republic, the state and the Church had worked closely together and the Church was involved in national matters like education.

2) Some prominent Nazis were anti-Christian and Nazi ideology disagreed with the role the Church had traditionally had in society.

3) Hitler thought religion should comply with the state and wanted churches to promote Nazi ideals. He was also worried that some members of the Church might publicly oppose Nazi policies.

4) The Nazi Party was careful to maintain support from the Catholic and Protestant Churches during its rise to power because they were so popular. However, as Hitler consolidated his totalitarian state, his control over churches increased.

The Catholic Church was Persecuted

1) In July 1933, an agreement called the Concordat was signed between the Pope and the Nazi government. Hitler promised not to interfere with the Catholic Church if the Church agreed to stay out of German politics.

2) The Catholic Church was now banned from speaking out against the Nazi Party, but Hitler soon broke his side of the deal.

> **Comment and Analysis**
> The Concordat reassured Christians that Hitler was consolidating ties with the Catholic Church, but he was actually restricting its power.

- The Nazi Party started to restrict the Catholic Church's role in education.
- In 1936 all crucifixes were removed from schools and by 1939 Catholic education had been destroyed.

- The Nazis began arresting priests in 1935 and put them on trial.
- Catholic newspapers were suppressed and the Catholic Youth group was disbanded.

3) In 1937, the Pope spoke out against Hitler in a letter to Catholic Churches in Germany. The stance of the Church had changed, but many German Catholics were too scared to speak out against the Nazi Party.

> Catholics tried to protect their religion by avoiding confrontation with the Nazi Party.

The Nazi Party Controlled the Protestant Church

The Protestant Church was reorganised and fell under Nazi control.

1) When Hitler became Chancellor in 1933, there were 28 independent Protestant Churches. These Churches were politically divided — some formed a group known as the 'German Christians'. They supported Hitler and favoured an anti-Semitic version of Christianity.

2) The Nazi Party backed this version of Christianity and believed all Christians should follow its principles. In 1936 all Protestant Churches were merged to form the Reich Church.

> **The Reich Church 'Nazified' Christianity...**
> The Reich Church replaced the symbol of a cross with the Nazi Swastika, and the Bible was replaced by 'Mein Kampf' (see p.24). Only Nazis could give sermons and the Church suspended non-Aryan ministers.

> **Comment and Analysis**
> Not everyone supported the Reich Church — it was opposed by a Protestant group called the 'Confessing Church' (see p.48).

3) The Reich Church was an attempt to increase state control over the Protestant Church and make a National Socialist version of Christianity.

Attitudes Towards the Church

Now that you know all about the Nazi Party's attitude towards the Church, have a go at these activities.

Thinking Historically

The Protestant and Catholic Churches were both powerful forces in German society. Because of this, the Nazi Party saw them as a threat and tried to gain control over Christianity in Germany.

1) Copy and complete the mind map below, giving reasons why each of the factors in the green boxes made the Church seem like a threat to the Nazi Party. Give as much detail as you can.

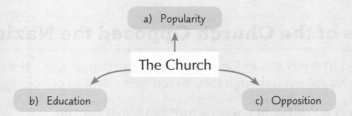

2) Which of the factors above do you think made the Church seem most threatening to the Nazi Party? Explain your answer.

Knowledge and Understanding

In an attempt to remove any risk of opposition, the Nazi Party put measures in place to control both the Catholic and Protestant Churches.

1) In your own words, explain what the Concordat was.
2) Did Hitler and the Catholic Church have similar or different reasons for signing the Concordat? Explain your answer.
3) Copy and complete the table below, listing the changes the Nazi Party made to the Catholic and Protestant Churches.

Catholic Church	Protestant Church

4) Explain how the Nazis' policies towards the Church helped to increase their control over German society.

The Nazis wanted the state to come first...

You might get sources in the exam that give different viewpoints on Nazi religious policies. Don't forget that Catholic and Protestant Christians were treated differently by the Nazis.

Opposition

The Nazis had a tight grip on Germany, but some opposition remained.

The Political Left opposed Hitler, but was Divided and Weak

1) Once in power, the Nazis had banned other political parties, including those on the political left, such as the Communist Party (KPD) and the Social Democratic Party (SPD).

2) But their members formed underground groups to try and organise industrial unrest (e.g. strikes). These networks were often infiltrated by the Gestapo (secret police), and party members could be executed.

3) Their impact was also limited because the different parties of the left were divided and didn't cooperate.

Some members of the Church Opposed the Nazis

There was little opposition to the Nazis in Germany from Christian groups. But a number of Church members did oppose the Nazis, even though they risked being sent to concentration camps:

1) Martin Niemöller was a Protestant pastor, a former U-boat captain, and a one-time Nazi supporter. He objected to Nazi interference in the Church, and was one of the founders of the Confessing Church. He used a sermon in 1937 to protest against the persecution of Church members, and as a result spent several years in concentration camps.

> The Confessing Church protested against Hitler's attempt to unite the different Protestant Churches into one Reich Church (see p.46).

2) Another key member of the Confessing Church was Dietrich Bonhoeffer, a Protestant theologian and pastor who opposed the Nazis from the beginning. He joined the resistance, helped Jews escape from Germany and planned an assassination of Hitler. He was caught and imprisoned, then executed just weeks before the fall of the Nazis.

3) Clemens August von Galen was the Catholic Bishop of Münster, who used his sermons to protest against Nazi racial policies and the 'euthanasia' of the disabled. His protests didn't stop the killing, but they did force the Nazis to keep them secret. Only the need to maintain the support of German Catholics stopped the Nazis from executing him.

The Edelweiss Pirates and Swing Kids were Youth Movements

1) The Edelweiss Pirates was the name given to groups of rebellious youths who rejected Nazi values and opposed the Hitler Youth organisation (see p.52).
   - They helped army deserters, forced labourers and escaped concentration camp prisoners.
   - At first the Nazis mostly ignored them, but cracked down after they started distributing anti-Nazi leaflets. Many members were arrested, and several were publicly hanged.

2) The Swing Kids (or Swing Youth) were groups of young people who rebelled against the tight control the Nazis had over culture, acting in ways considered 'degenerate' by the Nazi regime (e.g. listening to American music and drinking alcohol). They were mostly considered a nuisance rather than a threat, but some members were arrested and even sent to concentration camps.

Comment and Analysis

German opposition to the Nazis didn't really threaten their dominance, but it did mean the Gestapo was kept busy tracking down people who had distributed anti-Nazi leaflets, held secret meetings, committed acts of sabotage, etc.

Comment and Analysis

Other Germans expressed their dissatisfaction with the Nazi regime in 'low level' ways — e.g. by grumbling about the government or spreading rumours. Not everyone considers this genuine opposition, but even this was probably risky.

Opposition

Even though the Nazi Party had a lot of support and controlled most aspects of German society, some figures and groups dared to speak out against them. This page will help you get to grips with the facts.

Knowledge and Understanding

Members of the groups given below actively opposed Nazi control.

1) Copy and complete the mind map, giving details about each group, how they resisted the Nazis and how the Nazis responded to them.

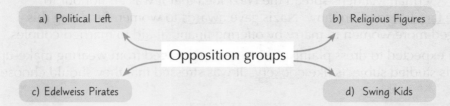

a) Political Left

b) Religious Figures

Opposition groups

c) Edelweiss Pirates

d) Swing Kids

Interpretation

The extract below is from a book on European history by James Joll.
It discusses opposition to the Nazi Party.

> Any open opposition [was] almost impossible and even any clandestine* resistance very difficult. Most protests of necessity remained personal — a furtive** act of friendship to a Jew, secret listening to foreign broadcasts, the passing on of a subversive*** joke or rumour... Above all, however, what made opposition or resistance hard was the knowledge that a majority of the German people had gone along with Hitler and had, if only for a time, wanted what he did.

*secret   **hidden   ***rebellious

1) What is Joll's main argument about the extent of opposition in Nazi Germany?
   Find a detail from the source which supports your answer.

2) Use the table below to help you structure an essay explaining how far you agree with Joll's main argument. Each row should represent a paragraph of your essay.

Point	Evidence	Why evidence supports point
Ordinary Germans did oppose the Nazis in a variety of different ways.	Underground political groups tried to organise strikes. Several members of the Church, such as Martin Niemöller and Dietrich Bonhoeffer, stood up to the Nazis. Youth groups like the Edelweiss Pirates spread anti-Nazi leaflets and rebelled against some aspects of Nazi rule.	The range of opposition from different groups in society shows that opposition to the Nazis wasn't as rare as Joll suggests.

Add three rows to the table to plan three more paragraphs.

Make sure you include arguments both for and against Joll's argument.

You can use evidence from the rest of the book to back up your points.

If you weren't with the Nazis, you were against them...

You need to be able to write about the different groups and figures who opposed the Nazis. Make sure you know their names, what they did and whether there were any consequences.

Life in Nazi Germany, 1933-39

Work and Home

The Nazis encouraged <u>women</u> to be <u>homemakers</u> and tried to provide <u>jobs</u> for <u>men</u>.

Women were expected to raise Large Families

1) Nazis didn't want <u>women</u> to have too much freedom. They believed the role of women was to provide <u>children</u> and support their families <u>at home</u>.

2) Women were <u>banned</u> from being <u>lawyers</u> in 1936, and the Nazis did their best to stop them following other professions.

3) The <u>League of German Maidens</u> spread the Nazi idea that it was an honour to produce <u>large families</u> for Germany. Nazis gave <u>awards</u> to women for doing this and encouraged more women to marry by offering <u>financial aid</u> to married couples.

4) Women were expected to dress plainly and were discouraged from wearing make-up and smoking. At school, girls studied subjects like <u>cookery</u>. It was stressed that they should choose '<u>Aryan</u>' <u>husbands</u>.

> A <u>shortage of workers</u> after 1937 meant more women had to <u>go back to work</u>.

> The Nazis taught that the ideal '<u>Aryan</u>' German was <u>tall</u> with <u>blonde hair</u> and <u>blue eyes</u>.

Public Works and Rearmament meant Unemployment Fell

1) Hitler started a huge <u>programme</u> of <u>public works</u>, which helped to reduce unemployment — e.g. from 1933 jobs were created as a result of the construction of <u>autobahns</u> (motorways).

2) <u>All</u> men between 18 and 25 could be <u>recruited</u> into the <u>National Labour Service</u> and given jobs.

3) Industrial output increased and <u>unemployment</u> fell.

4) Hitler also brought in <u>military conscription</u> and encouraged German <u>industry</u> to manufacture more <u>ships</u>, <u>aircraft</u>, <u>tanks</u> and <u>weapons</u> for the military. This <u>rearmament</u> meant further falls in <u>unemployment</u>.

5) Trade Unions were banned (see p.34), so workers had to join the Nazis' <u>Labour Front</u> instead. But workers <u>weren't allowed</u> to go on <u>strike</u> or campaign for better conditions, and <u>wages</u> were relatively <u>low</u>.

> **Comment and Analysis**
>
> Although <u>unemployment fell</u> after the Depression, the Nazis <u>fiddled</u> with the <u>statistics</u> to make it look lower than it really was — e.g. they didn't count <u>women</u> or <u>Jewish</u> people without jobs. The official unemployment statistics <u>didn't include</u> this invisible unemployment.

Many groups in society Felt Better Off

1) The Nazis made efforts to maintain the support of German <u>workers</u>. They wanted workers to feel <u>important</u> and believe that they were an essential part of the <u>Volksgemeinschaft</u>.

> '<u>Volksgemeinschaft</u>' means a <u>community</u> of people working hard towards the same <u>aims</u>.

- The Nazis introduced '<u>Strength through Joy</u>' — a scheme which provided workers with <u>cheap holidays</u> and leisure activities.
- The scheme also involved the introduction of the <u>Volkswagen</u> (the 'people's car') as a luxury people could aspire to own.
- The '<u>Beauty of Labour</u>' scheme encouraged factory owners to <u>improve conditions</u> for workers.

© Mary Evans / SZ Photo / Scherl

2) Many members of the <u>middle classes</u> also felt <u>better off</u> — e.g. small-business owners were able to advance more in society than previously.

3) But even though many people felt better off, workers and small-business owners had <u>lost out</u> in some ways.
- The cost of living rose by about <u>25%</u> — but wages didn't go up.
- Workers didn't have the <u>right</u> to <u>strike</u> or <u>resign</u>.
- <u>Small businesses</u> had to pay <u>high taxes</u>.

> **Comment and Analysis**
>
> During the <u>Depression</u>, one third of all workers had been <u>unemployed</u>. Many Germans had been <u>desperate</u>, so life under the Nazis did feel genuinely <u>better</u> for them.

Work and Home

Nazi social policies benefited many people, but they were also methods of control. The Nazis wanted to make sure that they could influence every aspect of people's lives — both at home and at work.

Thinking Historically

1) Copy and complete the table below, giving the positive and negative effects of the Nazi policies covered on page 50 for each group.

Group	Positive effects	Negative effects
a) **Women**		
b) **Unemployed people**		
c) **Workers**		
d) **Middle classes**		

2) Using your completed table to help you, explain why some Germans felt that their quality of life improved under the Nazis.

Source Analysis

The source on the right is a Nazi propaganda poster produced in the 1930s. It shows an eagle (a symbol of Nazi Germany) behind a family. The text can be translated as 'The Nazi Party secures the Volksgemeinschaft. People of the national community — if you need advice or help, then turn to the local group'.

© Glasshouse Images / Alamy Stock Photo

1) Write down two things that you can infer from this source about each of the points below. Give a detail from the source to back up each of your answers.

a) The Nazi view of the 'ideal' German family.
b) The role of the Nazi Party in German society.
c) The Volksgemeinschaft in Nazi Germany.

Imagine that you are using this source for an investigation into the role of women in Germany in the 1930s.

2) How does the purpose of the source affect its usefulness for your investigation?

Hitler reduced unemployment — and gained popularity...

It's important to use examples from your own knowledge to back up your answers in the exam. Learning the names of the schemes and associations on page 50 will help you to do this.

Life in Nazi Germany, 1933-39

Young People

An important key to Nazi success was controlling the minds of German youth.

Youth Movements helped produce Committed Nazis

1) Hitler knew that loyalty from young people was essential if the Nazis were to remain strong.

2) Youth movements were a way of teaching children Nazi ideas —
so they would be loyal to the Nazi Party when they grew up.

The Hitler Youth seemed exciting...
- The Hitler Youth was founded in 1926. Boys aged fourteen and over were recruited to the movement. It became all but compulsory in 1936 and lasted until 1945.
- Boys wore military-style uniforms and took part in physical exercise preparing for war. High-achieving boys might be sent to Hitler Schools to be trained as loyal Nazi leaders.
- They also went on camping trips and held sports competitions. Some of those who took part said the organisation was fun, made them feel valued and encouraged a sense of responsibility.

The League of German Maidens was for girls...
- The League of German Maidens was the female branch of the Hitler Youth, aimed at girls aged between fourteen and eighteen.
- Girls were trained in domestic skills like sewing and cooking.
- Sometimes they took part in physical activities like camping and hiking. This gave girls new opportunities that were normally reserved for boys.

Comment and Analysis

After 1936, all other youth organisations were banned and it was almost impossible for children to avoid joining the Hitler Youth. However, towards the end of the 1930s, attendance actually decreased as activities adopted an increasingly military focus.

Education across Germany was 'Nazified'

1) Education in schools meant learning Nazi propaganda. Most teachers joined the Nazi Teachers' Association and were trained in Nazi methods. Children had to report teachers who did not use them.

2) Subjects were rewritten to fit in with Nazi ideas. Children were taught to be anti-Semitic (i.e. prejudiced against Jews) — for example, Biology courses stated that Jews were biologically inferior to 'Aryans'. History courses explained that the First World War was lost because of Jews and communists.

3) Physical education became more important for boys to prepare them for joining the army. They sometimes even played games with live ammunition.

4) In universities, students burned anti-Nazi and Jewish books, and Jewish lecturers were sacked. Jewish teachers were also dismissed from public schools.

German children were always being bombarded with Nazi propaganda. Erika Mann, a German who opposed the Nazis, described Nazi education in Germany. 'Every child says 'Heil Hitler!' from 50 to 150 times a day...[it] is required by law; if you meet a friend on the way to school, you say it; study periods are opened and closed with [it]... [The Nazis'] supremacy over the German child...is complete.'

German Youth eventually became involved in Fighting the War

1) During the Second World War, members of the Hitler Youth contributed to the war effort — for example, helping with air defence work, farm work and collecting donations for Nazi charities.

2) Towards the end of the war, many Hitler Youth members ended up fighting alongside adults. They were known for being fierce and fanatical fighters.

Comment and Analysis

The Nazis' attempts to impose their ideology on children weren't always effective. See p.48 for more about how unofficial youth movements resisted Hitler and the Nazis.

Life in Nazi Germany, 1933-39

Young People

The Nazis controlled most aspects of young people's lives — check you've got to grips with all the details.

Source Analysis

The source below is a poster about the Hitler Youth. It was produced in 1936.

a) The poster uses military imagery, such as flags and drums.

c) This can be translated as 'Out with all the troublemakers!'

d) Hitler Youth members are shown as being big, powerful and serious.

b) Ordinary people seem tiny and scared. They are running away from the Hitler Youth.

e) This can be translated as 'Unity of young people in the Hitler Youth!'

1) Explain what you can infer about the way the Nazis portrayed the Hitler Youth from each detail in the blue boxes above.

2) What effect do you think this poster would have had on young people? Use details from the source to support your answer.

3) In the boxes below, there are three possible investigations about the Hitler Youth. Which investigation do you think this source would be most useful for? Explain your choice.

a) What was life like for members of the Hitler Youth?

b) How popular was the Hitler Youth in the 1920s?

c) Why did the Hitler Youth appeal to some young people?

4) Why do you think the source would be less useful for the other two investigations?

Thinking Historically

1) Copy and complete the table below, listing ways that the German education system was 'Nazified' and explaining why you think each change was introduced.

'Nazification' of education	Reason

The Hitler Youth — not everyone's favourite youth group...

When you're analysing a source, it's useful to think about the impact it was intended to have when it was first produced — what message was it supposed to give to its audience?

Life in Nazi Germany, 1933-39

Nazi Discrimination

The Nazi belief in the idea of a 'master race' caused a huge amount of harm.

Hitler wanted to 'Cleanse' Germany of 'Inferior' groups

1) Most Nazis believed that Germans were members of a superior ancient race called the 'Aryans'. Hitler thought people who were not pure Aryans (e.g. Jews) did not belong in Germany, and had no part to play in the new German Empire.

2) He wanted to 'cleanse' the German people by removing any groups he thought 'inferior'. Jews were especially targeted, but action was also taken against other groups.

> Hitler always claimed the Jews were responsible for many of Germany's problems.

- Many Romani ('gypsies') and Slavs (an ethnic group from central and eastern Europe) were sent to concentration camps. The Nazis believed that they were racially inferior.
- The Nazis murdered or sterilised many people who had mental and physical disabilities.
- Many people of mixed race were also sterilised against their will.
- Homosexual people were sent to concentration camps in their thousands. In 1936 Himmler, Head of the SS, began the Central Office for the Combating of Homosexuality and Abortion.

Nazis Changed the Law to Discriminate against Jews

1) In April 1933, the SA organised a national boycott of Jewish businesses, which resulted in Nazi-led violence against Jews. The violence wasn't popular with the German people, so the Nazis decided to use the legal system to persecute Jews instead.

2) Over time, the number of jobs that Jews were banned from gradually increased.

3) The Nuremberg Laws of 1935 were based on the idea that Jews and Germans were biologically different. They removed many legal rights from Jews and encouraged 'Aryan' Germans to see them as inferior.

- The Nuremberg Laws stopped Jews being German citizens.
- They banned marriage between Jews and non-Jews in Germany.
- They also banned sexual relationships between Jews and non-Jews.

> Some Jews were given passports enabling them to leave Germany but preventing them from returning.

4) Jews were later forced to close or sell their businesses, and they were banned from all employment.

5) By 1938, all Jewish children had been banned from attending German schools and Jews were no longer allowed in many public places, including theatres and exhibitions.

Comment and Analysis

The Nazis' racial policies aimed to isolate Jews from the rest of society. 'Aryan' Germans were even encouraged to break off friendships with Jews and avoid any contact with Jewish people.

Kristallnacht 1938 — the 'Night of the Broken Glass'

1) In November 1938, a German diplomat was murdered in Paris by a Jew.

2) There was anti-Jewish rioting throughout Germany — thousands of Jewish shops were smashed and almost every synagogue in Germany was burnt down. In the days that followed, thousands of Jews were arrested and sent to concentration camps.

3) The Nazis claimed that the events of Kristallnacht were a spontaneous reaction by the German people to the Paris murder. In fact, they had been planned and organised by the Nazi government. Few ordinary Germans had participated.

Comment and Analysis

Kristallnacht was a turning point in the Nazi persecution of Jews — it was the first widespread act of anti-Jewish violence in Nazi Germany. After Kristallnacht, conditions for German Jews got even worse.

Nazi Discrimination

Discrimination in Nazi Germany intensified over time. Test out what you know with the activities below.

Knowledge and Understanding

Between 1933 and 1939, conditions in Germany became gradually worse for Jews.

1) Make a timeline for the period 1933-39, showing all the main developments in the Nazis' persecution of Jewish people. Try to include as much detail as possible.

Source Analysis

The extract below is taken from an interview with a German woman called Helga Schmidt. Helga was not from a Jewish family, but she witnessed the changing treatment of Jewish people in Nazi Germany. The interview took place around 50 years after the fall of the Nazis.

> At first, we shopped in Jewish stores, probably because they were less expensive than other stores. But then they closed little by little... Signs were taped on the windows and doors of the Jewish shops and department stores saying "Jew" and so on, and we didn't trust ourselves anymore to shop there because it was said that we were being watched. And we believed that.

1) Imagine you are using this source for an investigation into the impact of the Nazi Party's anti-Semitic policies. Explain how each feature of the source listed below affects its usefulness for your investigation.

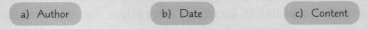

    a) Author   b) Date   c) Content

Interpretation

This interpretation is from a book by Marion A. Kaplan about life for Jews in Nazi Germany, published in 1998. She discusses the aftermath of the national boycott of Jewish businesses in April 1933.

> Many Germans who had been angered or embarrassed by the boycott on April 1 and had shown courage on that day tended to retreat* into privacy thereafter. They gradually submitted to the pressures of the "racial community", remaining silent rather than defending Jews... customers who were loyal at first began to dwindle** as the government increased its attack on Jewish businesses.

*withdraw **fade away

1) What is Kaplan's main argument about why Jewish people became increasingly isolated in Nazi Germany? Write down one detail from the interpretation to support your answer.

2) How does the interview with Helga Schmidt above support Kaplan's argument? Use details from both extracts to support your answer.

Nazi Germany — a climate of cruelty and fear...

In the exam, you might have to refer to sources and interpretations within the same answer. Think about the differences between them or whether they express similar points of view.

Life in Nazi Germany, 1933-39

Worked Exam-Style Questions

These worked answers will help you to tackle the tricky interpretations questions at the end of the exam.

Interpretation 1

At the same time as coercing the German people into conformity, measures were taken to attempt to obtain their consent to, and support for, the new national socialist community… In contrast to the uncertainties and hardship of the Weimar years, the Nazi dictatorship was associated for many Germans with a secure income and an improved standard of living, however qualified by restrictions on personal freedom.

An extract from a history book about Germany by Mary Fulbrook, published in 1997.

Interpretation 2

Not content with taking over all branches of government, and then of the state, the NSDAP [the Nazis] had taken power over the agencies of civil society. As a result, there was almost no association which people could join or activity in which they could engage that was not a branch of the NSDAP or in some way sponsored by, administered by or monitored by Nazis.

An extract from a history textbook about Germany by Nick Pinfield, published in 2015.

Look at Interpretations 1 and 2, which give different opinions about what life was like in Germany after Hitler came to power. Explain the main difference between the two opinions. [4 marks]

Identify the main opinion given in each interpretation.

Interpretation 1 suggests that the social and economic benefits of Nazi rule meant that life in Germany improved for many, despite the lack of freedom people experienced. The author claims that Nazi rule brought 'a secure income and an improved standard of living' and argues that overall, Nazi policies were viewed positively when compared to 'the uncertainties and hardship of the Weimar years'.

Use phrases like 'in contrast' to show you're comparing the interpretations.

In contrast, Interpretation 2 suggests that life in Germany was worse under the Nazis. The author argues that people's freedom was severely restricted due to the Nazis' 'power over the agencies of civil society'. He highlights the fact that every aspect of people's social and professional lives was overseen by the state.

Use evidence from the interpretations to back up your points.

Worked Exam-Style Questions

Give one reason why Interpretations 1 and 2 might express different opinions about what life was like in Germany after Hitler came to power.   [4 marks]

The interpretations are only partial extracts from longer pieces of writing, so the historians might focus on different aspects of the same issue.

Just focus on one reason why the interpretations express different views.

    One reason why the interpretations might express different opinions is that they are partial extracts. Each interpretation focuses on a different aspect of life in Nazi Germany.
    Interpretation 1 deals only with the positive changes made by the Nazi Party. It emphasises the fact that for many, the standard of living in Germany improved, particularly in comparison to the Weimar years. The author mentions the coercion and 'restrictions on personal freedom' that Nazi rule brought, but doesn't elaborate on these in this extract.
    On the other hand, Interpretation 2 focuses solely on how the Nazis controlled society and people's lives. To demonstrate the negative consequences of Nazi rule, the author writes about people's lack of freedom and the way that German society was 'monitored by the Nazis'. He doesn't mention any of the positive changes introduced by the Nazi Party in this extract.

Use evidence from the interpretations to support your answer.

You can write about what the interpretations don't include if it helps.

Worked Exam-Style Questions

To what extent do you agree with the opinion expressed in Interpretation 1 about what life was like in Germany after Hitler came to power? You should refer to both interpretations and use your own knowledge to support your answer.   [16 marks]

For questions like this in the exam, 4 extra marks will be awarded for spelling, punctuation, grammar and using specialist terminology.

You should state your <u>understanding of the interpretation</u> at the beginning.

Interpretation 1 argues that, although people faced 'restrictions on personal freedom' after Hitler came to power, many Germans had a positive attitude towards the Nazis, because the party ensured that people had 'a secure income and an improved standard of living'. Although I agree that life improved for some Germans under the Nazis, in general I disagree with Interpretation 1, because I think that the negative aspects of the Nazis' social policies outweighed the positive ones.

It's important to <u>summarise</u> your <u>argument</u> in the <u>introduction</u>.

For many Germans, the early years of Nazi rule seemed to be better than the 'hardship of the Weimar years', as Interpretation 1 argues. In Depression-era Germany, one third of the entire workforce was unemployed at one point. This figure was drastically reduced under Nazi rule due to the introduction of public works projects, such as the construction of new autobahns, the creation of the National Labour Service (which offered employment to all men between the ages of 18 and 25) and the programme of state rearmament. Particularly by addressing the unemployment crisis, the Nazi Party made some positive economic changes which improved the standard of living for many people in Germany, as Interpretation 1 suggests.

Use your <u>own knowledge</u> to help you decide whether the interpretation is <u>convincing</u> or <u>not</u>.

Interpretation 1's claim that the standard of living improved under the Nazis is also supported by many of the social policies the party introduced. Schemes like 'Strength through Joy', which provided workers with benefits such as cheap holidays and leisure activities, meant that life improved for many working people. Hitler's concept of Volksgemeinschaft also encouraged Germans to work towards the same aims as a community and made people feel like they were valued by the state. Therefore, it is hardly surprising that many Germans who had felt betrayed and let down by the politicians who ran the Weimar Republic associated Nazi rule with positive improvements in their lives.

Use <u>technical terms</u> from the period to demonstrate your <u>knowledge</u> of the topic.

Make sure you discuss arguments <u>both for and against</u> the interpretation.

However, as Interpretation 2 shows, the Nazis' social policies were also intended as methods of coercion and control — they went hand in hand with the Nazis' efforts to take over 'all branches of government, and then of the state'. For example, the 'Strength through Joy' scheme might have offered

Worked Exam-Style Questions

people cheap holidays, leisure activities and cars but, as Interpretation 2 points out, schemes like this were also methods of ensuring that almost every aspect of life in Germany was 'sponsored by, administered by or monitored by' the Nazis. This coercive element is even clearer in other policies aimed at workers, such as the Nazis' decision to outlaw Trade Unions and instead force all workers to join the Nazis' Labour Front, or their withdrawal of the right to strike or resign. The coercive aspects of the Nazis' social policies suggest that, while these policies may have achieved some positive changes for workers and other groups in society, they didn't necessarily improve people's overall standard of living as Interpretation 1 suggests.

While there may be some debate about whether certain groups in society benefited from Nazi rule, it cannot be denied that there were people for whom life clearly got much worse under the Nazis. For Jewish people and other ethnic or social groups who were persecuted by the Nazis, life in Nazi Germany was extremely difficult. The Nuremberg Laws of 1935 are a clear indication of how life in Nazi Germany became increasingly unbearable for Jewish people — Jews were described as biologically inferior to 'Aryans', were no longer classed as German citizens and were stripped of many legal rights. By 1939, Jewish people, homosexuals, disabled people and other minority groups were being sent to concentration camps in huge numbers. For those groups excluded from Hitler's concept of Volksgemeinschaft, therefore, life under the Nazis was clearly not better than it had been during the Weimar Republic, something that is not acknowledged by Interpretation 1.

Although I agree that some Germans benefited from the social and economic changes the Nazis introduced, overall I disagree with the view expressed in Interpretation 1. The author of Interpretation 1 suggests that the lives of many Germans improved under the Nazis despite 'the restrictions on personal freedom', but I would agree with Interpretation 2's view on the oppressive nature of life in Nazi Germany. Restrictions on people's personal freedom often made everyday life worse, as citizens felt controlled, intimidated and restricted by the Nazis. Any perceived positive changes were achieved at the expense of many vital freedoms.

Remember to refer to both interpretations in your answer.

To get top marks, you need to analyse the interpretations in detail.

Including specific details like dates shows good knowledge of the topic.

When you give evidence, make sure you explain how it supports your argument.

Remember to answer the question directly in the conclusion.

Life in Nazi Germany, 1933-39

Exam-Style Questions

Here are some more exam-style questions for you to have a go at.

Source A

An extract from a book by Alfons Heck, a boy who grew up under the Nazi regime. It was published in 1985.

As soon as the Nazi regime came into power, it revamped the educational structure from top to bottom, and with very little resistance... We five- and six-year-olds received an almost daily dose of nationalistic instruction, which we swallowed as naturally as our morning milk. It was repeated endlessly that Adolf Hitler had restored Germany's dignity and pride and freed us from the shackles of Versailles... Even in working democracies, children are too immature to question... what they are taught by their educators.

Source B

A song sung by a youth group called the Navajos, who were a part of the Edelweiss Pirates. They were opposed to Nazi rule.

Hitler's strength makes us small,
We are still lying in chains.
But we will be free again one day,
We are going to break the chains.
For our fists are strong,
Yes, and our knives are ready,
The Navajos fight
For young people's freedom.

Interpretation 1

An extract from a journal article, published in 2015.

Few governments in history were more ambitious in their attempt to indoctrinate the population than the Nazi regime in Germany, and it particularly focused on the young... beliefs of Germans in their first decades of life were strongly malleable* [and so] propaganda and schooling were highly effective in changing attitudes and beliefs of those growing up under the Nazis... Nazi propaganda and schooling increased the number of youngsters who became fervent** anti-Semites.

*easy to influence   **passionate

Exam-Style Questions

Interpretation 2

An extract from a history textbook aimed at secondary school pupils, published in 2016.

> Towards the end of the 1930s, some young people began to question the Nazi regime. Many teenagers rejected the values taught in the Hitler Youth and formed their own youth groups instead. One such group, the Edelweiss Pirates, had many local chapters across Germany; its members actively opposed the Nazis, sometimes coming into conflict with Hitler Youth members. This rebellion came with a price — in 1944, leading members of the Cologne branch of the Edelweiss Pirates were executed by the Nazis to send a message to other independent-minded young people. Despite this brutality, teenagers still signed up to oppose the Nazis through these groups.

Exam-Style Questions

1) Explain how useful Sources A and B are for an investigation about how successfully the Nazis controlled young people in Germany. Use both sources, as well as your own knowledge, to support your answer.   [8 marks]

2) Look at Interpretations 1 and 2, which give different opinions about how successfully the Nazis controlled young people in Germany. Explain the main difference between the two opinions.   [4 marks]

3) Give one reason why Interpretations 1 and 2 might express different opinions about how successfully the Nazis controlled young people in Germany. You can refer to Sources A and B to support your answer.   [4 marks]

4) To what extent do you agree with the view expressed in Interpretation 1 about how successfully the Nazis controlled young people in Germany? You should refer to both interpretations and use your own knowledge to support your answer.   [16 marks]

For questions like this in the exam, 4 extra marks will be awarded for spelling, punctuation, grammar and using specialist terminology.

Life in Nazi Germany, 1933-39

Exam-Style Questions

Source C

A photograph from the 1930s, showing a group of Jewish men being made to carry a large Star of David* through the streets.

© Historic Collection / Alamy Stock Photo

*a Jewish symbol

Exam-Style Questions

5) Infer two things from Source C about the treatment of Jews in Nazi Germany. Explain each inference that you make. [4 marks]

6) Explain why the Nazi Party tried to control the Church in Germany. You could mention education and religious opposition in your answer, but you should also use your own knowledge. [12 marks]

Answers

<u>Marking the Activities</u>

We've included sample answers for all the activities. When you're marking your work, remember that our answers are just a <u>guide</u> — a lot of the activities ask you to give your own <u>opinion</u>, so there is <u>no 'correct answer'</u>. The most important thing is that your answers use <u>accurate</u>, <u>relevant</u> information about the period and are <u>clearly explained</u>.

<u>Marking the Exam-Style Questions</u>

For each exam-style question, we've covered some <u>key points</u> that your answer could include. Our answers are just <u>examples</u> though — answers very different to ours could also get top marks.
Just remember, you can only gain marks for things that are <u>relevant</u> to the question.

Most exam questions in history are <u>level marked</u>. This means the examiner puts your answer into one of several <u>levels</u>. Then they award <u>marks</u> based on how well your answer matches the description for that level.

To reach a higher level, you'll need to give a '<u>more sophisticated</u>' answer. Exactly what 'sophisticated' means will depend on the type of question, but, generally speaking, a more sophisticated answer could include <u>more detail</u>, <u>more background knowledge</u> or make a <u>more complex judgement</u>.

Here's how to use levels to mark your answers:

1. Start by choosing which <u>level</u> your answer falls into — there are <u>level descriptions</u> at the start of each answer.
   - Pick the level description that your answer matches <u>most closely</u>. If different parts of your answer match different level descriptions, then pick the level description that <u>best matches</u> your answer as a whole.
   - A good way to do this is to start at 'Level 1' and <u>go up to the next level</u> each time your answer meets <u>all</u> of the conditions of a level. For example, if your answer meets all of the conditions for 'Level 3', but it has a few bits that match the description for 'Level 4', then choose 'Level 3'.

2. Now you need to choose a <u>mark</u> — look at the <u>range of marks</u> that are available <u>within the level</u> you've chosen.
   - If your answer <u>completely matches</u> the level description, or parts of it match the <u>level above</u>, then give yourself a <u>high mark</u> within the range of the level.
   - If your answer mostly matches the level description, but some parts of it <u>only just match</u>, then give yourself a mark in the <u>middle</u> of the range.
   - Award yourself a <u>lower mark</u> within the range if your answer only just meets the conditions for that level or if parts of your answer only match the <u>level below</u>.

<u>The Weimar Republic, 1918-29</u>

Page 7 — The War Ends

Knowledge and Understanding

1 a) The Social Democratic Party and the Independent Social Democratic Party. Two socialist parties that declared a republic and formed Germany's temporary government.
  b) The ruler of the German Empire until November 1918.
  c) A country ruled with elected representatives instead of a monarch.
  d) The governments that dealt with local affairs in Germany's 18 states.
  e) A truce between opposing sides in a war.
  f) The name of the temporary national government set up after the Revolution.

2
  - Early November 1918 — Some members of the German navy rebel. In Hanover, troops refuse to control rioters. Kurt Eisner encourages a general uprising, which sparks mass strikes in Munich. A public protest is held in Berlin. Members of the SPD call for the Kaiser's resignation.
  - 9th November 1918 — Kaiser Wilhelm abdicates. The SPD and the USPD declare a republic.
  - 10th November 1918 — All the state leaders appointed by the monarchy leave their posts. New revolutionary state governments take over.
  - 11th November 1918 — Britain, France and the USA sign an armistice with Germany. WW1 ends.
  - January 1919 — Elections are held for a new Reichstag.

Thinking Historically

1 a) These prevented food and essential supplies from reaching Germany during the war. As a result, Germans did not have enough food and many suffered from starvation. This weakened people's faith in the Kaiser's leadership and caused unrest.
  b) Kaiser Wilhelm was unpopular by the end of the war. Many people no longer wanted a ruler who behaved like a king, so they pushed for a democracy.
  c) This weakened the Kaiser because it meant that he could no longer rely on the armed forces to support him. It also showed that there was no real hope of Germany winning the war.
  d) Eisner encouraged mass strikes, which made the Kaiser look weak.

2 You can choose any of the factors, as long as you explain your answer. For example:
  Allied naval blockades were the most important cause, because they prevented vital supplies from reaching Germany. This caused extreme hardship and even starvation for German people. As a result, people lost faith in the Kaiser and called for the war to end. If people hadn't been so hard hit by the Allies' tactics in the war, then Kurt Eisner's call for an uprising might not have been so effective and there might not have been disobedience in the military. The Allied naval blockades were therefore the root cause of many of Germany's other problems.

Answers

Page 9 — The Weimar Republic

Thinking Historically

1 a) • Strength — This made the electoral system fairer, as the proportion of seats a party received roughly matched their share of the vote.

b) • Strength — The system was very democratic because smaller parties were represented in the Reichstag, giving them a say in German politics.
• Weakness — There were lots of small parties with different points of view in the Reichstag. This made it difficult to make decisions.

c) • Strength — The public had greater power and women enjoyed more rights. More people could get involved in German politics.

d) • Strength — The President could take action when the Reichstag was unable to make a decision.
• Weakness — The new democracy was undermined by the President's ability to suspend the constitution.

Interpretation

1 a) The Weimar Constitution allowed more people to vote by extending the vote to anyone over the age of twenty. It also introduced proportional representation, which was a more democratic voting system. It allowed parties with as little as 0.4% of the vote to gain seats in the Reichstag.

b) Because he wants to suggest that the constitution didn't work very well in practice.

2 Shirer argues that the Weimar Constitution was admirable because it was very democratic and liberal. However, he implies that its main weakness was that it only worked 'on paper' and wasn't very effective in practice.

3 Here are some points your answer may include:
• Shirer's argument that the Weimar Constitution was very 'liberal and democratic' is supported by the fact that the vote was extended to include both men and women over the age of twenty.
• The use of proportional representation meant that the electoral system was very democratic, because even small parties could have a say in German politics.
• Shirer's suggestion that the new system only worked 'on paper' is supported by features such as Article 48, which undermined the democratic nature of the constitution by allowing the President to overrule the Reichstag.
• The system of proportional representation meant the political system didn't work well in practice. It was difficult for the Reichstag to make decisions and this encouraged the President to use Article 48.

Page 11 — Early Unpopularity

Knowledge and Understanding

1 • Article 231 forced Germany to take the blame for the war. — Germans felt humiliated by having to accept the full blame.
• Germany's armed forces were reduced to 100,000 men. They were banned from having armoured vehicles, aircraft or submarines and limited to six warships. — Germans felt vulnerable with such limited defences.
• Germany was forced to pay £6,600 million in reparations. — The reparations seemed unfair to Germans and damaged Germany's economy.
• Germany lost its empire. Its former colonies were put under the control of the League of Nations. — Germans

didn't like losing territory, especially when people in German colonies were forced to become part of a different nation.
• The German military was banned from the Rhineland. — Germans felt vulnerable because Germany was open to an attack from the west.

2 • Germans viewed the treaty as a 'Diktat' that had been forced on them by the Allies, and they resented the politicians who signed the treaty for giving in to the Allies' demands.
• Germans felt betrayed by the politicians because they believed that Germany could still have won the war, so it wasn't necessary for the politicians to agree to the treaty.

Source Analysis

1 b) Some Germans felt that the future of their country was now in the hands of Britain, France and the USA. The problems caused by the reparations weren't temporary but would continue to damage Germany in the future.

c) It seemed like the Allies didn't care how much harm they might cause Germany by squeezing as much money out of the Germans as they could.

d) Some Germans saw the reparations as a way of making the Allies rich at Germany's expense.

Page 13 — Years of Unrest

Knowledge and Understanding

1 a) The leaders of a group of communists. In January 1919, they led the Spartacist Revolt to try to take over Berlin.

b) Ex-German soldiers who helped to put down the Spartacist Revolt. In March 1920, some of them supported the Kapp Putsch, which tried to overthrow the Weimar regime.

c) The leader of the Kapp Putsch, which tried to overthrow the Weimar government and install a new right-wing government.

Interpretation

1 The author suggests that right-wing groups were the biggest threat to Weimar democracy. He argues that 'the danger of the extreme right' was 'the real growing threat to Weimar democracy'.

2 a) • The Kapp Putsch was organised by right-wing groups. This was a serious threat because it aimed to create a new right-wing government.
• Ebert made the Freikorps seem legitimate when he asked them to help put down the Spartacist Revolt. This made them more of a threat, giving them confidence to take part in the Kapp Putsch to overthrow the Republic.
• The divide between the Social Democratic Party and the communists weakened the left. This made them less of a threat to the Weimar Republic.

b) • The Spartacists led a revolt that managed to take control of important buildings in Berlin. This shows they were a genuine threat to the Weimar Republic.
• The Spartacist Revolt was supported by a large number of workers who went out on strike. This meant the left was able to put a significant amount of pressure on the Weimar Republic.
• The Kapp Putsch failed because the workers were opposed to the extreme right. This suggests a left-wing uprising was more likely to gain popular support than a right-wing one.

Answers

Thinking Historically

1 a) France and Belgium decide to take Germany's resources instead, so they occupy the Ruhr.

b) German industry is devastated and the government tries to solve the debt crisis by printing more money.

c) Germany's currency becomes worthless and Germany is unable to trade, so shortages of food and goods get worse.

Page 15 — Recovery

Knowledge and Understanding

1 a) 1924 — France and Belgium agreed to withdraw from the Ruhr. More realistic dates for paying back reparations were agreed. The USA lent Germany £40 million to help pay off its debts.

b) 1925 — Germany, France and Belgium agreed to respect their joint borders.

c) 1926 — Germany was allowed to join the League of Nations and was re-established as an international power.

d) 1928 — 66 countries, including Germany, agreed not to use violence to settle disputes.

e) 1929 — The Allies agreed to reduce the reparations to a quarter of the original amount. Germany was given 59 years to pay them.

2 Here are some points your answer may include:

• The reparations Germans had to pay were reduced, and they were given extra time and money to pay them back. This made Germany more financially stable.

• France and Belgium were forced to withdraw from the Ruhr. They also agreed to recognise their joint borders with Germany. This made Germany's borders more stable and secure.

• Germany built better international relationships as a result of the agreements and was allowed to join the League of Nations. This helped Germany to re-establish itself as an international power.

• Germany and many other countries promised not to use violence to settle disputes. This created stability by reducing the risk of another war breaking out.

Source Analysis

1 a) The source is from 1929. This makes it useful because it means Stresemann could look back on 1923-1929 and evaluate it as a whole. However, he might not have had a complete understanding of the economic situation, because some details of Germany's economic recovery might not have emerged until after the Wall Street Crash.

b) The source is from a speech to the League of Nations, so it tells us about how Stresemann wanted to present Germany's economic situation to other countries. However, the purpose of the speech means it might not give a completely accurate picture of Germany's economic situation. For example, Stresemann may have exaggerated the economic challenges faced by Germany in an attempt to convince other nations not to treat Germany too harshly.

c) The fact that the source is from a speech by Gustav Stresemann makes it useful because Stresemann was in a position to understand Germany's economic situation well. As Chancellor and Foreign Minister, he had played a central role in bringing about Germany's economic recovery. Stresemann's reputation was tied to the success of Germany's economic recovery. Therefore it is likely that he is expressing his genuine views, since he gives a negative assessment of the economic situation, despite the fact that doing so could harm his reputation.

d) The source is useful because it provides evidence that senior German politicians were already worried about the uncertain nature of Germany's economic recovery before the Wall Street Crash.

Page 17 — Changes Under the Weimar Republic

Interpretation

1 Interpretation 1 focuses on improving living conditions in Weimar Germany, whereas Interpretation 2 focuses on its economic and political problems.

2 The author of Interpretation 1 supports her argument by referring to increases in workers' wages, the benefits brought by house-building programmes, improvements to health care services and the increasing levels of welfare provision available. Interpretation 2 gives examples of Germany's wider problems, including the dependence of the German economy on loans from the USA, high unemployment levels and declining support for moderate political parties.

3 Here are some points your answer may include:

• Interpretation 1 gives a more positive impression of the Weimar Republic than Interpretation 2 because it focuses on a different aspect of life in the Weimar Republic. Interpretation 1 focuses almost entirely on improvements in living conditions, whereas Interpretation 2 focuses on Germany's wider political and economic problems.

• Interpretation 1 gives a more positive impression than Interpretation 2 because it is based on different evidence. Interpretation 1 uses statistics related to wage growth and house-building to reflect the improving living conditions in Germany, whereas Interpretation 2 is based on unemployment statistics and evidence showing a lack of support for moderate political parties.

Knowledge and Understanding

1 a) The government introduced unemployment insurance in 1927 and created more jobs with its mass housing projects.

b) Wages for industrial workers rose quickly in the late 1920s.

c) More than 2 million new homes were built between 1924 and 1931 due to the government's mass housing projects.

d) The role of women was changing, giving them new opportunities. Women were able to vote and could enter politics more easily. The number of young women working increased in the years after the war. New women's sports clubs and societies sprang up. Divorce also became easier.

e) The Weimar Republic encouraged freedom of expression, so new ideas were generated. Brecht and other cultural figures developed new styles, as drama, music, literature and cinema all started to change. New ways of critical thinking were encouraged and a cabaret culture developed in Berlin.

2 Here are some points your answer may include:

• 1924-1929 are often considered the 'Golden Years' of the Weimar Republic because more people were in work and they were receiving higher wages. Those who remained unemployed were also more protected thanks to the introduction of unemployment insurance.

Answers

- The housing situation improved in 1924-1929 due to a house-building project that spanned the period and carried on into the 1930s. This meant that millions more Germans were living in suitable accommodation.
- Women were granted new opportunities to take part in public life by working, voting and becoming elected themselves. Their lives improved in other ways, as they were able to join sports clubs and take part in a range of other leisure activities.
- 1924-1929 can be seen as 'Golden Years' for culture, because the Weimar Republic experienced cultural developments in many areas, such as drama, music, literature and cinema.

Pages 20-21 — Exam-Style Questions

1 This question is level marked. How to grade your answer:

Level 1 1-2 marks	The answer gives a simple analysis of the sources to come to a basic judgement about their usefulness for the investigation. It shows a basic understanding of the sources' content and/or provenance, as well as displaying some relevant knowledge of the topic.
Level 2 3-5 marks	The answer analyses the sources in more detail to make judgements about their usefulness for the investigation. It shows a good understanding of the sources' content and/or provenance and uses relevant knowledge to support its judgements.
Level 3 6-8 marks	The answer evaluates the sources to make judgements about their usefulness for the investigation. It shows a detailed understanding of the sources and uses relevant knowledge to analyse their content and provenance, and to support its judgements.

Here are some points your answer may include:
- Source A is useful because it shows what life was like for many German people towards the end of the First World War. It doesn't relate directly to Kaiser Wilhelm's abdication, but demonstrates that due to the Allied blockade, Germans faced a shortage of food. This contributed to Kaiser Wilhelm's abdication because it led to unrest and to public opinion turning against him.
- The usefulness of Source A is limited because it only shows a queue in a single place and at a single time. It doesn't show whether this happened regularly or took place anywhere else in Germany.
- Source B is useful because it was written by Kaiser Wilhelm himself, so it gives a first-hand account of his reasons for abdicating.
- Source B was written in 1922, after the armistice, the German Revolution and the Treaty of Versailles. This limits its usefulness, because the Kaiser's view was probably influenced by these events, so the source may not accurately reflect his reasons for abdicating in 1918.
- The usefulness of Source B is limited because it was published and available to the public. The Kaiser might have wanted to portray himself in a positive light or show people that he wasn't responsible for Germany's decline.

2 This question is level marked. How to grade your answer:

Level 1 1-3 marks	Limited knowledge and understanding of the period is shown. The answer gives a simple explanation of why the German economy experienced a recovery. Ideas are generally unconnected and don't follow a logical order.
Level 2 4-6 marks	Some relevant knowledge and understanding of the period is shown. The answer gives a basic analysis of some of the reasons why the German economy experienced a recovery. An attempt has been made to organise ideas in a logical way.
Level 3 7-9 marks	A good level of knowledge and understanding of the period is shown. The answer explores multiple reasons why the German economy experienced a recovery. It identifies some relevant connections between different points, and ideas are organised logically.
Level 4 10-12 marks	**Answers can't be awarded Level 4 if they only discuss the information suggested in the question.** Knowledge and understanding of the period is precise and detailed. The answer considers a range of reasons why the German economy experienced a recovery and analyses each one. All ideas are organised logically and connections between different points are identified to create a developed analysis of the topic.

Here are some points your answer may include:
- Stresemann took steps to fix the economy when he became Chancellor in August 1923. For example, his decision to end the strike in the Ruhr meant that the government no longer had to compensate striking workers.
- Stresemann's introduction of the Rentenmark in November 1923 helped the economy by replacing the failed German Mark and stabilising Germany's currency.
- Stresemann created a political coalition between moderate, pro-democracy socialist parties in the Reichstag to make it easier to pass legislation. This co-operation meant that decisions about the economy were no longer hindered by political differences.
- Stresemann made an effort to improve Germany's relationships with other countries when he was appointed Foreign Minister in November 1923. This approach led to agreements that addressed the problem of German war reparations. For example, the Dawes Plan (1924) made the repayment terms for Germany's reparations more realistic. The Young Plan (1929) reduced the reparations. This relieved pressure on the German economy.
- The Dawes Plan played a big role in helping the German economy to recover, since the USA lent money to Germany so that it could pay reparations to Britain and France. This gave Germans a chance to rebuild their economy as they were no longer struggling as much with reparations payments. The importance of the Dawes Plan is shown by the fact that the German economy collapsed again once the USA was no longer able to lend Germany money following the Wall Street Crash in 1929.

Answers

- The government's house building programme, which resulted in more than 2 million homes being built between 1924 and 1931, provided employment opportunities for Germans. This strengthened the economy as more Germans had a wage and could afford to spend money.

3 This question is level marked. How to grade your answer:

Level 1 1-2 marks	The answer gives a difference, but it is only loosely supported by reference to the interpretations.
Level 2 3-4 marks	The answer gives a key difference, which is well supported by reference to both interpretations.

Here are some points your answer may include:

- Interpretation 1 argues that the Weimar Republic was always doomed to fail. The author writes that 'the past and the future cast their shadows over Weimar's middle years', suggesting that there was no hope of lasting stability. On the other hand, Interpretation 2 argues that the fall of the Weimar Republic was not inevitable. It suggests that 'the Weimar government may well have continued to thrive if it weren't for the Wall Street Crash'.
- Interpretation 1 argues that even when the Weimar Republic seemed to experience 'prosperity' in the 1920s, it was actually unstable and weak because 'political instability persisted'. Interpretation 2 argues that the Weimar Republic really was prospering in the second half of the 1920s, as shown by 'the increased support for democratic parties in the 1928 elections'.

4 This question is level marked. How to grade your answer:

Level 1 1-2 marks	The answer gives a basic explanation of reasons why the interpretations are different. This is based on a simple analysis of the interpretations or on knowledge of the topic.
Level 2 3-4 marks	The answer gives a detailed explanation of reasons why the interpretations are different. This is well supported by a detailed analysis of the interpretations and knowledge of the topic.

Here are some points your answer may include:

- The authors might express different views because the interpretations are only partial extracts. Interpretation 1 focuses only on the long-term problems of the Republic in terms of its 'political instability', whereas Interpretation 2 focuses on the achievements of the Weimar Republic in 'addressing many of Germany's most pressing problems in the latter half of the 1920s'.
- The authors might express different views because they value the positive and negative aspects of the Weimar Republic differently. Interpretation 2 highlights the Weimar Republic's positive features, suggesting they would have outweighed its negatives, if not for the Wall Street Crash. Interpretation 1 emphasises the significance of the Republic's negative features, suggesting they would always overshadow its positive ones.

5 This question is level marked. How to grade your answer:

Level 1 1-4 marks	The answer either supports or disagrees with the interpretation. This is based on a simple analysis of one interpretation and basic knowledge of the topic.
Level 2 5-8 marks	The answer shows support or disagreement by evaluating the interpretation. The evaluation draws on analysis of both interpretations and some relevant knowledge of the topic. An overall judgement is made, but it isn't well supported by the answer.
Level 3 9-12 marks	The answer shows support or disagreement by evaluating the interpretation in detail. The evaluation draws on a detailed analysis of both interpretations, which considers their different viewpoints and shows a good level of relevant knowledge. An overall judgement is made that is partly supported by the answer.
Level 4 13-16 marks	The answer considers both sides of the argument. It draws on an accurate and detailed analysis of both interpretations, which considers their different viewpoints and shows an excellent level of relevant knowledge. An overall judgement is made that is well supported by the answer.

Here are some points your answer may include:

- Interpretation 1 argues that the Weimar Republic's stability was undermined by deep political divisions and a lack of 'political consensus'. This seems like an accurate description of the Weimar Republic's political difficulties. The Republic's system of proportional representation meant that lots of small parties had a say, and it was hard for the Reichstag to make decisions. As a result, political instability was written into the Weimar Constitution.
- Interpretation 1 describes how 'the past and the future cast their shadows over Weimar's middle years'. This is convincing as between 1919 and 1923, the Weimar Republic struggled with attempted uprisings, public outrage about the armistice and the Treaty of Versailles, and hyperinflation caused by the need to pay reparations. Then, in 1929, the Wall Street Crash caused the economy to collapse. With the benefit of hindsight, it is clear that even in its 'halcyon days', the Weimar Republic's apparent stability was precarious and couldn't last.
- Interpretation 1 implies that the Weimar Republic was always likely to fail, but there is evidence to suggest that the Republic was stable until the Great Depression in 1929. As Interpretation 2 points out, there was 'increased support for democratic parties in the 1928 elections'. This suggests that Weimar democracy really was working by 1928, and that the Republic was becoming increasingly stable. Therefore, if it weren't for the problems caused by the Wall Street Crash, the Weimar Republic might have survived.
- Interpretation 1 suggests that the Weimar Republic remained 'feeble and divided' throughout the 1920s. However, as Interpretation 2 argues, Weimar politicians did manage to address 'many of Germany's most pressing problems in the latter half of the 1920s'.

Answers

The Locarno and Kellogg-Briand pacts helped to improve Germany's international position, while the problem of reparations was improved by the Dawes and Young plans. During the 1920s, Germany's currency was stabilised and workers' wages and unemployment benefits improved. These positive economic changes demonstrate that the Weimar Republic had built a stable economic base by 1929.

- Interpretation 1 implies that the 'prosperity' of the 1920s was only an illusion. Yet Interpretation 2 convincingly argues that in many ways the Weimar Republic was thriving in the mid 1920s. Women's rights, living standards and cultural production all improved. These developments improved the Republic's political stability, as people would have been more willing to support a system that offered them a good standard of living.

Hitler's Rise to Power, 1919-33

Page 23 — Early Stages of the Nazi Party
Source Analysis
1 a) Hitler suggests that nationalism means being prepared 'even to die for' your country.
   b) He says that the Nazis intend to 'build up the State and the community'.
   c) He says that 'everyone who is a German at all has the same blood'.
   d) He argues that those who speak 'the same language' should be a 'single people'.
   e) He claims that the Nazis will show 'a boundless and all-embracing love for the people' and emphasises the importance of acting in the 'interest of the community'.
2 The language used in the speech might have made the Nazis seem appealing. Hitler's use of phrases such as 'community of the people' and 'boundless and all-embracing love' might have made the Nazis seem caring and encouraged people to think that the Nazis would be more supportive than the Weimar government, which many Germans felt betrayed by in 1922.

Thinking Historically
1 The Programme was intended to establish the identity of the Nazi Party. It was designed to appeal to as much of the German population as possible by promising to resolve most of the issues Germany was facing in the wake of the armistice and the Treaty of Versailles.
2 Here are some points your answer may include:
- Nationalists — The Nazis emphasised German greatness and promised to make Germany a strong country again. In his speech, Hitler said the Nazis were willing to 'die' for the German people and promised that they would 'build up the State'.
- People with anti-Semitic views — The Nazis had a strongly anti-Semitic message. Their Twenty-Five Point Programme said that Jews shouldn't be German citizens, and in his speech Hitler suggested that only those with 'the same blood' could be considered German.
- Elderly people — The Nazi Party promised to improve pensions.
- Middle classes — The Twenty-Five Point Programme specified that the middle classes should be supported and protected.

- Workers — The Nazis branded themselves as the National Socialist German Workers' Party. In the Twenty-Five Point Programme, they said that all German citizens should have a job.

Page 25 — The Munich Putsch
Interpretation
1 Interpretation 1:
- Main argument — The Munich Putsch caused Hitler to lose the support of some nationalist groups, who saw him as weak, disorganised and untrustworthy.
- Evidence — The revolt was quickly stopped by the police and never really looked like being successful. Support for the Nazis declined after the Putsch. The Nazi Party and the SA were banned, while Hitler went to prison until late 1924.

Interpretation 2:
- Main argument — The Munich Putsch had a positive influence on Hitler's political career, enabling him to spread his views more widely.
- Evidence — Hitler's trial after the Putsch gave him a public platform to spread his views. He wrote 'Mein Kampf' while in prison. This was key to spreading his ideology because it was read by millions of Germans.

2 You can choose either of the interpretations, as long as you explain your answer. For example:
Interpretation 2 is more convincing, because it is supported by more evidence and acknowledges both sides of the argument. The author of Interpretation 2 recognises that the Putsch was 'a disastrous failure' at first, but shows how it improved Hitler's reputation in the long run. Hitler's trial gave him a valuable chance to spread his ideas. His imprisonment allowed him to write 'Mein Kampf', which was read by many people and raised his status as a political leader. At a time when many Germans saw Weimar politicians as traitors to Germany, Hitler proved that he was willing to die for his country and his beliefs by attempting a coup.

Thinking Historically
1 a) At the Bamberg Conference in 1926, Hitler made it clear that the party would only follow his agenda.
   b) The party became more centralised. It adopted a national structure, with regional branches run by gauleiters. The gauleiters supervised local branches, but were controlled by the party leadership.
   c) Nazi propaganda increased and was centrally controlled by the party. Hitler re-established the SA in 1926 and used them for propaganda purposes.
   d) New organisations were established for different social groups. The Hitler Youth was founded in 1926, and the Nazis established organisations for different professions, such as the National Socialist Teachers' League.
2 a) Hitler's control over the party's agenda ensured that the party wouldn't be divided. While Weimar politicians appeared unable to decide anything, the Nazis would seem decisive and unified.
   b) The new, more centralised structure gave Hitler greater control over the party and a broader influence across Germany as a whole. The party was more organised and operated more efficiently.
   c) Increased propaganda helped the Nazis to spread their views more widely. By taking central control of the Nazis' propaganda, Hitler ensured that the Nazis' message would be communicated consistently throughout Germany.

d) The creation of new organisations helped the Nazis to attract voters from many different sections of society and helped to persuade people that the Nazis would protect their interests.

Page 27 — The Great Depression
Thinking Historically
1 a) • International economic crisis — The USA can no longer afford to prop up the German economy. The USA suspends future payments and asks for old loans to be repaid. (Economic)
   • Germany's economy collapses — Industrial production goes into decline; factories and banks shut down. (Economic)
   • Germany is affected by mass unemployment. (Social)
   b) • Chancellor Brüning is appointed to deal with the crisis. (Political)
   • Brüning increases the cost of imported food to help German agriculture, but food prices rise as a result. (Economic)
   • Brüning cuts government salaries and pensions. He increases taxes and reduces unemployment benefits. (Economic)
   • Brüning cuts back social services. (Social)
   • Living conditions in Germany get worse under Brüning. (Social)
   • People become dissatisfied with the government and Brüning loses support in the Reichstag. (Political)
   c) • Brüning has to use Article 48 regularly and asks President Hindenburg to suspend the constitution so that he can make decisions without parliamentary approval. (Political)
   • The German people feel neglected by the government and begin to look towards extremist political parties. (Political)
2 Possible answers are shown in brackets above.
3 You can choose any of the options, as long as you explain your answer. For example:
   Economic consequences were the most significant because they caused the social and political problems. The withdrawal of US loans and the collapse of the German economy made living conditions in Germany desperate. They forced the government to impose unpopular economic and social policies, which could only be passed using undemocratic measures such as Article 48. The economic consequences of the Wall Street Crash made it impossible for the Weimar Republic to succeed politically or socially.

Source Analysis
1 The date is significant because the source was created for the election campaign in 1932, at the height of the Great Depression. It therefore provides evidence of how the social and economic difficulties during the Depression shaped the messages used by the Nazis to gain support from German voters.
2 This makes the source useful because it provides evidence of some of the messages the Nazis used in order to appeal to voters. However, the fact that the source is a propaganda poster also limits its usefulness, because the source doesn't show how people responded to these messages and whether they were an important factor in the appeal of the Nazi Party.
3 The artist might have chosen to include the words 'work', 'freedom' and 'bread' to show that the Nazis would

solve the problems created by the Great Depression. Unemployment was very high by 1932, so the Nazis promised to create more jobs. The economic problems also meant that some people were struggling to afford food, so the Nazis promised them 'bread'. Many Germans felt that they lacked 'freedom' by 1932, because of the use of undemocratic measures like Article 48, so the Nazis promised people greater freedom.

Page 29 — The Rise of the Nazis
Knowledge and Understanding
1 • Green line — Social Democratic Party (SPD)
   • Red line — Communist Party of Germany (KPD)
   • Black line — Nazi Party
2 • The SPD's share of votes dropped quite sharply in 1930, before decreasing more steadily between 1930 and November 1932. They lost support in every election.
   • Votes for the KPD increased steadily and consistently between 1928 and November 1932.
   • The Nazi Party saw a huge increase in support from 1928 to July 1932. They suffered losses in the November 1932 election, but remained very popular.
3 Extremist parties became more popular in Depression-era Germany because the population was becoming increasingly desperate. The failure of Weimar politicians to address the problems caused by the Depression led many people to support parties that promised more extreme solutions.

Source Analysis
1 The Nazis included people from different groups in order to win support from throughout society in the election. They wanted to show that their policies would benefit a wide range of people.
2 The poster suggests that life in the Weimar Republic was very dismal and depressing. This is shown by the dull colours and the unhappy expressions on the people's faces. The poster also suggests that life in the Weimar Republic was hopeless — the text implies that Hitler was the only person who could make people's lives better.
3 By emphasising the misery and hopelessness of life in the Weimar Republic, the Nazis implied that a radical change was necessary. They wanted to demonstrate that only the Nazis could make life better for the German people.
4 The Nazis were popular with voters in 1932 because they capitalised on the feelings of despair and hopelessness that existed in Germany as a result of the Great Depression. At a time when democratic politicians seemed powerless to solve Germany's social and economic problems, the Nazis promised to bring about a dramatic change that would improve things for every group in society.

Page 31 — Hitler Becomes Chancellor
Knowledge and Understanding
1 • April 1932 — Economic conditions in Germany are getting worse. Presidential elections take place, with Hindenburg and Hitler standing. Despite being confident of winning, Hindenburg only gets a majority in the second ballot, where he wins 53% of the vote.
   • May 1932 — Chancellor Brüning is dismissed and Franz von Papen is appointed in his place.
   • July 1932 — The Nazi Party performs well in the election and becomes the most popular party in the Reichstag. Hindenburg refuses to make Hitler Chancellor because he doesn't trust him.

- November 1932 — The Nazi Party loses 34 seats in the federal election.
- December 1932 — Hindenburg replaces Papen with Kurt von Schleicher as Chancellor. Schleicher offers the role of Vice-Chancellor to a leading Nazi, Gregor Strasser, in an attempt to divide the Nazis. However, Hitler stops Strasser from accepting. Papen is convinced that Schleicher pushed him out of government and wants to get back in. He makes a deal with Hitler — Papen will persuade Hindenburg to make Hitler Chancellor, as long as Hitler then makes Papen Vice-Chancellor.
- January 1933 — Papen persuades Hindenburg to make Hitler Chancellor.

Interpretation

1   Interpretation 1 argues that Hindenburg's mistakes were the most important factor in the fall of the Weimar Republic. Hindenburg is described as the 'undertaker of the Republic' who dug 'Weimar's grave'. Interpretation 2 suggests that the Great Depression was responsible for the fall of the Weimar Republic. It states that the Weimar Republic 'could have survived' were it not for the mass unemployment and unrest the Depression brought.

2   The sources support the main argument made in Interpretation 2 because they provide evidence of how the Nazis exploited the social and economic consequences of the Great Depression to gain votes in elections. For example, the poster on page 27 focuses on the Nazis' promise to bring people 'work', 'freedom' and 'bread', which are shown as answers to the problems of unemployment, poverty and political instability caused by the Depression. Similarly, the poster on page 29 suggests that Hitler is the 'last hope' for people who have been negatively affected by the Depression.

3   Here are some points your mind maps may include:
    Interpretation 1
    - Hindenburg beat Hitler in the presidential election in 1932. This demonstrates that he had popular support and didn't have to make Hitler Chancellor.
    - Hindenburg was the only person who could legally appoint Hitler as Chancellor and had refused to do so in 1932. If he had continued to refuse, it would have been impossible for Hitler to become Chancellor by legal means.
    - Hindenburg underestimated the threat that Hitler posed — he believed that Hitler could be controlled like a puppet.
    Interpretation 2
    - Interpretation 2 uses election results to support its claim that, before the Depression, extremist parties like the Nazis were not a significant political force and that democratic parties were gaining in popularity. The 1928 election results in particular suggest that most German people supported democracy before the Great Depression. This suggests that the Depression was central to the fall of the Weimar Republic.
    - Extremist parties like the Nazis won support by promising to tackle many of the effects of the Great Depression, such as unemployment and the fall in the standard of living. Nazi propaganda from the early 1930s is focused on combatting the problems people were facing during the Depression.

- The Depression made the Weimar Republic less democratic, because Brüning used measures like Article 48 to pass his unpopular social and economic policies. This contributed to the fall of the Weimar Republic by making extremist, anti-democratic parties like the Nazis seem more acceptable and less of a threat.
- People who had suffered during the Depression felt angry and wanted someone to blame. This made the Nazis' anti-Semitic and anti-communist views more appealing, because they provided scapegoats for Germany's economic problems.

Page 33 — Exam-Style Questions

1   This question is level marked. How to grade your answer:

Level 1 1-3 marks	Limited knowledge and understanding of the period is shown. The answer gives a simple explanation of why the Great Depression weakened support for the Weimar Republic. Ideas are generally unconnected and don't follow a logical order.
Level 2 4-6 marks	Some relevant knowledge and understanding of the period is shown. The answer gives a basic analysis of some of the reasons why the Great Depression weakened support for the Weimar Republic. An attempt has been made to organise ideas in a logical way.
Level 3 7-9 marks	A good level of knowledge and understanding of the period is shown. The answer explores multiple reasons why the Great Depression weakened support for the Weimar Republic. It identifies some relevant connections between different points, and ideas are organised logically.
Level 4 10-12 marks	**Answers can't be awarded Level 4 if they only discuss the information suggested in the question.** Knowledge and understanding of the period is precise and detailed. The answer considers a range of reasons why the Great Depression weakened support for the Weimar Republic and analyses each one. All ideas are organised logically and connections between different points are identified to create a developed analysis of the topic.

Here are some points your answer may include:
- By agreeing to foreign loan schemes like the Dawes Plan, Weimar politicians made the German economy reliant on the USA. When the Wall Street Crash occurred and the German economy suffered as a result, it's likely that the population would have blamed the Weimar government. This would have weakened support for the Republic.
- The collapse of the German economy caused widespread unemployment. Many Germans blamed the government for its inability to solve this problem and support for the Weimar Republic weakened as a result.
- Chancellor Brüning introduced economic policies which made living conditions in Germany worse for many people. They caused food prices and taxes to rise and some salaries and unemployment benefits to fall. This made the Weimar Republic less popular because people blamed Brüning and the government for the fall in living conditions.

- Many of Brüning's policies were so unpopular that he had to use Article 48 in order to pass them. The German population felt that the Weimar Republic was no longer behaving as a democracy and their views were not being represented. This turned many people against the Weimar Republic because they felt betrayed by the system.
- When it became clear that the Weimar government wasn't working, people began to look to alternative parties who might offer something different. Parties like the Nazis and the KPD used the Depression as a way of highlighting the Weimar Republic's failings and converted many people to their cause. Support for the Weimar Republic fell as people who had once supported democratic parties began to support extremist ones instead.

2 This question is level marked. How to grade your answer:

Level 1 1-2 marks	The answer gives a difference, but it is only loosely supported by reference to the interpretations.
Level 2 3-4 marks	The answer gives a key difference, which is well supported by reference to both interpretations.

Here are some points your answer may include:
- The main difference is that Interpretation 1 argues that Hitler's 'personal power' was responsible for the growing popularity of the Nazis — the Nazi Party became more popular because Hitler managed to stand out from the 'faceless politicians' he was standing against. In contrast, Interpretation 2 argues that it was the social and economic conditions of Weimar Germany during the Depression that caused the growing popularity of the Nazis. The Nazi Party needed 'exactly the conditions' created by the Depression in order to become so popular.
- The main difference is that Interpretation 1 argues that it was Hitler himself and his personality as a great leader that made the Nazis so popular. The German people believed that 'salvation' could only come from Hitler. In contrast, Interpretation 2 argues that it was the Nazi Party's policies and ideas — their 'hatred and perverted patriotism' — which caused their growth in popularity.

3 This question is level marked. How to grade your answer:

Level 1 1-2 marks	The answer gives a basic explanation of reasons why the interpretations are different. This is based on a simple analysis of the interpretations or on knowledge of the topic.
Level 2 3-4 marks	The answer gives a detailed explanation of reasons why the interpretations are different. This is well supported by a detailed analysis of the interpretations and knowledge of the topic.

Here are some points your answer may include:
- The authors express different views because the interpretations are partial extracts and focus on different aspects of the question. Interpretation 1 focuses on Hitler's charisma and leadership. Interpretation 2, on the other hand, focuses on the social and economic reasons behind the rise in Nazi support.
- The authors express different views because they have used different evidence. Interpretation 2 uses evidence from Christopher Isherwood, who provides a first-hand account about living conditions in Berlin.

Interpretation 1 considers Hitler's character, so might be drawing on evidence more specifically related to Hitler, such as his speeches or accounts from people who met him.

4 This question is level marked. How to grade your answer:

Level 1 1-4 marks	The answer either supports or disagrees with the interpretation. This is based on a simple analysis of one interpretation and basic knowledge of the topic.
Level 2 5-8 marks	The answer shows support or disagreement by evaluating the interpretation. The evaluation draws on analysis of both interpretations and some relevant knowledge of the topic. An overall judgement is made, but it isn't well supported by the answer.
Level 3 9-12 marks	The answer shows support or disagreement by evaluating the interpretation in detail. The evaluation draws on a detailed analysis of both interpretations, which considers their different viewpoints and shows a good level of relevant knowledge. An overall judgement is made that is partly supported by the answer.
Level 4 13-16 marks	The answer considers both sides of the argument. It draws on an accurate and detailed analysis of both interpretations, which considers their different viewpoints and shows an excellent level of relevant knowledge. An overall judgement is made that is well supported by the answer.

Here are some points your answer may include:
- Interpretation 2 claims that the economic and social problems caused by the Wall Street Crash were vital to the Nazis' popularity. Election results from 1928 and 1932 support this argument — in 1928, before the Wall Street Crash, the Nazis won just 3% of the vote, but in July 1932 they won 37%. This suggests that the social and economic conditions in Germany after the Great Depression were a key factor in the growing popularity of the Nazis after 1929.
- Interpretation 2 argues that the Nazi Party grew in popularity because it offered 'hope of national renewal'. This is convincing because many of the Nazis' policies were based on restoring Germany's power. The bright future the Nazis promised in their Twenty-Five Point Programme would have been appealing in Depression-era Germany because many of the problems Germany had faced in the early 1920s still hadn't been solved by 1929, and the Depression had also created new problems.
- Interpretation 2 refers to the high levels of unemployment that existed in Berlin during the Depression, arguing that this contributed to the Nazis' growth in popularity. In October 1929, 1.6 million people in Germany were out of work, rising to over 6 million by February 1932. The Nazis exploited this unemployment crisis to attract support, using their propaganda and policies to offer the unemployed and those who feared for their jobs a brighter and more secure future.
- Interpretation 2 argues that it was the Nazis as a party who were able 'to convince voters that Hitler's own brew of dictatorship, hatred and perverted patriotism' was right for Germany. This is convincing because the

Answers

success of the Nazis relied on many different features of the party. For example, the SA played an important part in the Nazis' success — they held demonstrations and distributed propaganda. The party was also successful in elections because it was well structured and organised — for example, gauleiters were appointed to oversee regional branches of the party, and efficient, effective propaganda campaigns ran throughout Germany.

- Interpretation 2 doesn't comment on the significance of Hitler's personality and charisma for the Nazis' growth in popularity. This makes Interpretation 2 less convincing because Hitler's appeal as a strong leader and great speaker played a key part in the growing popularity of the Nazis after 1929. As Interpretation 1 argues, Hitler's 'personal power' as leader appealed to many because it made him stand out from the 'faceless politicians' who opposed him.
- Interpretation 1 argues that Hitler's promise to take '*personal* responsibility' for solving Germany's problems was a key reason for the Nazis' growing popularity. This is convincing because many Germans felt betrayed by ineffective Weimar politicians by 1929. Far from solving the crisis of the Great Depression, Brüning's economic policies seemed to make everyday life worse for many Germans — he was so unpopular that he even became known as the 'Hunger Chancellor'. Hitler, by contrast, engaged with the German people on a personal level and promised to take responsibility for 'sweeping away the causes of the misery' which Weimar politicians had failed to do.

Nazi Control and Dictatorship, 1933-39

Page 35 — Achieving Total Power
Thinking Historically
1
- In early 1933, the Nazis use their control of the media to prevent other parties from carrying out effective campaigns. Opposition meetings are banned.
- In February 1933, the SA raids the Communist Party headquarters and claims to have found evidence that the communists are planning an uprising.
- Six days before the March 1933 elections, the Reichstag building catches fire. The Nazis blame the communists and try to spread anti-communist feelings by publishing anti-communist conspiracy theories in their newspapers.
- Hitler is given emergency powers by Hindenburg, which he uses to imprison members of the Communist Party and intimidate communist voters.
- In March 1933, Hitler makes the Communist Party illegal in order to gain control of the Reichstag.
- Hitler passes the Enabling Act, which allows him to govern without Parliament. He uses these powers to ban all political parties apart from the Nazi Party.

Interpretation
1 Here are some points your answer may include:
- Point — The Reichstag fire was an important turning point because it led to Hitler being given emergency powers, which made it easier for the Nazis to intimidate and suppress the communists.
- Evidence — Under the emergency powers, many basic rights, such as freedom of speech, were suspended. Hitler used the emergency powers to intimidate communist voters and imprison communist members.

- Why evidence supports point — This helped Hitler consolidate his power because it weakened the Communist Party. It made it harder for them to campaign in elections and may have made some people scared to vote for them. It also increased support for the Nazis among anti-communist voters because it showed that the Nazis were dealing with the communist 'threat'.
- Point — Hitler's decision to ban the Communist Party was more important than the Reichstag fire because it gave the Nazis control of the Reichstag.
- Evidence — As Interpretation 2 points out, the Nazis didn't win an absolute majority in the March 1933 elections. The Nazis only gained control of the Reichstag by banning the Communist Party, which had 81 seats.
- Why evidence supports point — Despite the Nazis' campaign of intimidation after the Reichstag fire, the communists remained an opposition force capable of winning a significant number of votes. Banning the Communist Party was therefore more important for Hitler's consolidation of power than the Reichstag fire, because it was the step that eliminated the communists as political opponents.
- Point — The Enabling Act was a more important factor than the Reichstag fire because it allowed Hitler to pass controversial legislation that was essential for his consolidation of power.
- Evidence — Hitler used the Enabling Act to ban Trade Unions in May 1933 and to ban all other political parties in July 1933.
- Why evidence supports point — This gave Hitler complete political control and silenced most opposition, which made it very difficult for anyone to challenge the Nazis' grip on power.

Page 37 — Achieving Total Power
Interpretation
1
- Point — The 'Night of the Long Knives' was more important than the Reichstag fire in Hitler's consolidation of power because it eliminated the main threat to Hitler from within the Nazi Party.
- Evidence — The SA was a threat because its members had become more loyal to Ernst Röhm than to Hitler. On 29th-30th June 1934, Hitler had many leading members of the SA killed or imprisoned.
- Why evidence supports point — This helped consolidate Hitler's power because it stamped out all potential opposition from within his party and demonstrated that he was prepared to act ruthlessly against anyone who opposed him. After the 'Night of the Long Knives', Hitler was in complete control of the Nazi Party.
- Point — Hitler's power wasn't fully consolidated until he reorganised the system of government to allow himself to control Germany from above.
- Evidence — Hitler created the role of Führer, which combined the previously separate posts of Chancellor, President and Commander-in-Chief of the army. Hitler's new system of government gave the Nazis control on both a national level (the reichsleiters) and a local level (the gauleiters).

Answers

- Why evidence supports point — Until Hitler reorganised the system of government, he was still effectively operating within the Weimar system. The reorganisation of government cemented his position as a dictator and gave him great power to influence the lives of Germans on both a national and local level.

Knowledge and Understanding

1 • The Führer — Hitler's role as supreme leader of the country. A combination of the posts of President, Chancellor and Commander-in-Chief of the army.
   • Reichsleiters — Advisers to Hitler, such as Goebbels and Himmler.
   • Gauleiters — Loyal Nazis who were each in charge of a 'Gau' (a province of Germany).
   • Other Officials — These included local and district party leaders.

2 Hitler's reorganisation of government helped him to achieve total power, because it gave him control over all aspects of life in Germany. The structure of the new system made it clear that Hitler was in overall charge, and ensured that his policies were effectively carried out on both a national and regional level.

Source Analysis

1 a) The fact that the source is a speech made by Hitler himself makes it useful, because Hitler would know exactly why he organised the 'Night of the Long Knives'. However, its usefulness is limited because Hitler probably wasn't giving a complete and accurate account of his reasons in the speech — he would have wanted to present the 'Night of the Long Knives' in a way that would serve his goal of gaining complete control over Germany.

  b) The date of the source makes it useful to the investigation, because the speech was given less than two weeks after the 'Night of the Long Knives', so it reveals how Hitler explained the events very soon after they took place. However, the speech was made at a time when Hitler was still consolidating his power and trying to win support for the Nazis, so it's likely that he would have tried to present his reasons for the attack on the SA in a way that made it seem justified.

  c) The source comes from a speech to the Reichstag so the purpose of the speech might be to convince the members of the Reichstag that he had acted rationally and was justified in arresting and killing members of the SA. This might limit its usefulness, because it's unlikely that Hitler would have spoken openly and honestly in this context.

  d) The content of the source makes it useful, because Hitler is directly addressing the question of why he organised the 'Night of the Long Knives'. He claims that the SA were no longer following his orders and instead were attempting to serve 'other tasks or interests'. This provides evidence that Hitler felt threatened by the SA and planned the 'Night of the Long Knives' to eliminate that threat.

Page 39 — The Machinery of Terror

Knowledge and Understanding

1 • The Law for the Reconstruction of the Reich — Gave the Nazis power over local governments.
   • Control of the civil service — Civil servants who didn't support the Nazis could be sacked.
   • Changes to the legal system — Special courts were set up in 1933 where the basic rights of those on trial were suspended. From 1934, people were tried for political crimes at the People's Court in Berlin and almost always found guilty. This made it easier for the Nazis to remove anyone who tried to oppose them.
   • Changes to judges' guidelines — Judges no longer had to be 'fair' or 'unbiased', but were expected to make rulings in line with Nazi policy. This allowed the Nazis to punish anyone who disagreed with their ideas.
   • The Sicherheitsdienst (SD) — This intelligence service aimed to keep people under constant supervision.
   • The Schutzstaffel (SS) — Helped to protect Hitler and intimidated people with their cruelty.
   • The Gestapo — The secret police. They used harsh interrogations and imprisonment without trial to make people afraid to oppose the Nazis.
   • Local wardens — Employed to keep watch over local people and ensure they were loyal to the Nazis.
   • Public participation — The public were encouraged to participate in the police state by reporting on each other.
   • Concentration camps — Used to imprison political prisoners and others who were seen as a threat.

Interpretation

1 • 'popular approval' — Peukert suggests that many people in Germany supported the Nazis' use of terror.
   • 'highly visible' — According to Peukert, the actions of the police state were clear for everyone to see.
   • 'approved and welcomed' — Peukert claims that many Germans were glad that the Nazis were persecuting certain social groups.

2 Interpretation 1 argues that the police state mostly operated in secret, describing it as a 'shadow'. The author suggests that people were afraid of the police state.

3 The argument of Interpretation 2 is different because Peukert argues that the actions of the police state were clear for the public to see — Peukert says that the terror 'was highly visible'. In contrast to Joll, he argues that the public approved of the police state.

4 The arguments might be different because the interpretations are partial extracts. Interpretation 1 only discusses 'the terror' in general terms, without distinguishing between features that affected everyone and features that only affected certain groups. On the other hand, Interpretation 2 focuses on 'specific manifestations of terror' targeted at particular groups. The author doesn't consider aspects of the police state that might have affected the population more generally.

Page 41 — Propaganda

Source Analysis

1 a) • Hitler has a large crowd of supporters behind him.
     • Most of the people in the crowd are waving Nazi flags.
  b) • The text says 'Long Live Germany!' suggesting that the Nazis would help Germany.
     • Hitler is portrayed like a religious leader, with the light of heaven shining down on him. This suggests that he would lead the German people towards a better life.
     • Hitler is shown leading the Germans into battle.
  c) • Hitler is the biggest figure in the picture, standing at the front of the crowd.
     • Hitler looks strong and defiant, ready to lead the large crowd behind him into battle.
     • The people in the crowd are saluting Hitler, demonstrating their loyalty to him.

Answers

2   I think the source would be most useful for investigation b) because it is a Nazi poster, so it provides direct evidence of some of the messages the Nazis included in their propaganda.

3
- The source would be less useful for investigation a) because the source can only tell us about the image of Hitler that the Nazis wanted people to see — it doesn't provide any evidence about what he was actually like as a leader.
- The source would not be very useful for investigation c) because it can't tell us how effective Nazi propaganda was. We don't know how people responded to the poster or if it had any effect on their attitudes.

Knowledge and Understanding

1   Joseph Goebbels was in charge of the Nazis' 'propaganda machine'. He founded the Ministry of Public Enlightenment and Propaganda in 1933 and was responsible for developing the 'Hitler Myth'.

2 a) Propaganda — Spreading information to promote a certain point of view, with the aim of influencing how people think and behave.

   b) Censorship — Preventing people from seeing or hearing certain pieces of information.

3
- The Nazis would unite Germany and make it strong.
- Germans should hate the countries that signed the Treaty of Versailles and support foreign expansion.
- Hitler was the saviour of Germany.
- Jews and communists were responsible for Germany's problems.
- Germans should return to traditional values.

4
- Censorship — The Nazis prevented Germans from seeing or hearing anything that gave a different message to their own propaganda.
- Radio — The Nazis sold cheap radios and controlled all the broadcasts, enabling them to reach most ordinary people in their homes.
- Newspapers — The Nazis gradually took control of German newspapers, so that they could decide what was published in them.
- Films — The Nazis produced films showing the strength of the Nazis and how weak their opponents were.
- Posters — Nazi posters spread messages about how evil the Nazis' enemies were and told Germans how to live their lives.

Page 43 — Propaganda

Thinking Historically

1
- Public rallies — The Nazis used rallies to spread their ideas and demonstrate their strength.
- Sporting events — Events like the Berlin Olympics were used to show off German wealth and power.
- Art and architecture — The Nazis constructed grand new buildings to demonstrate the strength and power of Germany. They banned modern art and promoted traditional German artists and musicians instead.

- Education — The Nazis rewrote school textbooks and children were taught Nazi ideas at school.
- The 'Strength through Joy' programme — The Nazis used this to persuade ordinary workers that they cared about their standard of living.

2
- The Nazis would unite Germany and make it strong. — This might have been appealing because many people felt that Germany had been weak in the Weimar years and that it needed to be strong in order to defend its interests abroad and compete internationally.
- Germans should hate the countries that signed the Treaty of Versailles and support foreign expansion. — Many Germans saw the Treaty of Versailles as a 'Diktat' forced on them by the Allies. They wanted to get back the territory that had been 'stolen' under the Treaty.
- Hitler was the saviour of Germany. — After the division and weakness of the Weimar years, many Germans wanted a strong leader who would take control.
- Jews and communists were responsible for Germany's problems. — Some Germans already had anti-Semitic or anti-communist beliefs, so they found this message appealing.
- Germans should return to traditional values. — Many Germans thought the Weimar Republic had been too liberal, so they welcomed a return to traditional values.

Source Analysis

1 b) The source is useful because Haffner lived in Germany under the Nazis, so he witnessed Nazi propaganda first hand. He was writing from Britain, so he probably wasn't afraid to express his opinion honestly. The source provides useful evidence for the power of Nazi propaganda because even someone like Haffner, who probably had strong anti-Nazi beliefs, thought that it was effective.

   c) Haffner lived in Germany for most of the 1930s and wrote this source soon after he left. This makes it useful because it means his comments are based on his recent experience of several years of Nazi propaganda.

2 a) The source is useful because it shows that the Nazis aimed to make propaganda that would appeal directly to ordinary people. However, its usefulness is limited because it doesn't tell us anything about whether they actually achieved this.

   b) Goebbels was in charge of Nazi propaganda, so he would understand better than anyone else how the Nazis tried to make their propaganda effective. However, because he was a leading figure in the Nazi Party, it is unlikely that he would criticise Nazi propaganda, so the source probably doesn't give a balanced view of its effectiveness.

   c) The source was written in 1931 at a time when the Nazis were developing their methods of propaganda, so it is useful for understanding the early ideas behind Nazi propaganda methods. However, the source is not that useful for understanding the effectiveness of Nazi propaganda later in the 1930s because Nazi propaganda continued to change and develop after 1931.

Answers

Page 45 — Exam-Style Questions

1 Each inference is marked separately. You can have up to two marks per inference. How to grade your answer:
- 1 mark for giving one credible inference.
- 2 marks for giving one credible inference and using content from the source to back it up.

Here are some points your answer may include:
- The forces of the Nazi police state watched over ordinary people. The woman describes how they 'were kept under surveillance.'
- The police state employed different tactics, such as working undercover, to ensure their enquiries were effective. The secret police came to the woman's apartment dressed 'in civilian clothes'.
- Even tiny details were checked up on by the forces of the police state — the source explains that the secret police checked that people were saying 'Heil Hitler'.
- The Nazi police state encouraged people to inform on each other. The secret police went to the woman's landlord and asked about her.

2 This question is level marked. How to grade your answer:

Level 1 1-2 marks	The answer gives a simple analysis of the sources to come to a basic judgement about their usefulness. It shows a basic understanding of the sources' content and/ or provenance, as well as displaying some relevant knowledge of the topic.
Level 2 3-5 marks	The answer analyses the sources in more detail to make judgements about their usefulness. It shows a good understanding of the sources' content and/or provenance and uses relevant knowledge to support its judgements.
Level 3 6-8 marks	The answer evaluates the sources to make judgements about their usefulness. It shows a detailed understanding of the sources and uses relevant knowledge to analyse their content and provenance, and to support its judgements.

Here are some points your answer may include:
- Source A is useful because it explains how the police state worked. It provides some evidence of how the Nazi Party controlled the population, and how these forces of terror became part of everyday life under the Nazis.
- Source A is useful because it shows an ordinary German's experiences of how the Nazis tried to control her life. The woman being interviewed lived under the Nazi regime and witnessed the police state first hand.
- Source A is useful because the interview took place a long time after the end of the Nazi regime, so the interviewee would not have been worried about speaking freely about Nazi control.
- The usefulness of Source A is limited because the interview took place a long time after the events it describes, so it is possible that the interviewee might have mis-remembered details or been influenced by what she had subsequently learnt about Nazi Germany.

- Source B is useful because it was produced during Nazi rule, so it gives an insight into how people at the time understood the methods the Nazis used to control the population. It shows that people at the time believed that the Nazi Party controlled the population by using members of the public as part of the police state.
- Source B is useful because it was created by an artist who lived in Nazi Germany, so it may have been based on his first-hand experience of Nazi methods of control.
- Source B is useful because it suggests that the police state created an atmosphere of fear and suspicion. This may have helped the Nazis to control people by influencing their behaviour and encouraging them to conform.
- Source B is limited in its usefulness because it was produced by an artist who was involved in resistance against the Nazis, and so must have held anti-Nazi views. The cartoon might exaggerate the truth about Nazi control in order to suit the artist's beliefs.

3 This question is level marked. How to grade your answer:

Level 1 1-3 marks	Limited knowledge and understanding of the period is shown. The answer gives a simple explanation of why Nazi propaganda was effective. Ideas are generally unconnected and don't follow a logical order.
Level 2 4-6 marks	Some relevant knowledge and understanding of the period is shown. The answer gives a basic analysis of why Nazi propaganda was effective. An attempt has been made to organise ideas in a logical way.
Level 3 7-9 marks	A good level of knowledge and understanding of the period is shown. The answer explores multiple reasons why Nazi propaganda was effective. It identifies some relevant connections between different points, and ideas are organised logically.
Level 4 10-12 marks	**Answers can't be awarded Level 4 if they only discuss the information suggested in the question.** Knowledge and understanding of the period is precise and detailed. The answer considers a range of reasons why Nazi propaganda was effective and analyses each one. All ideas are organised logically and connections between different points are identified to create a developed analysis of the topic.

Here are some points your answer may include:
- The Nazis used a wide range of methods to spread their propaganda, including the media, posters, films, art and spectacular events and displays. This meant that people were exposed to propaganda in all areas of their lives.
- The Nazis used censorship to control the media. By 1939, 70% of German households had a radio. Since the Nazis controlled radio broadcasts, many Germans were exposed to Nazi propaganda through the radio. The Nazis also had increasing control of German newspapers. This ensured that most Germans only heard and read Nazi points of view, as the Nazis were able to censor the media and control what was said.

Answers

- Goebbels' 'propaganda machine' repeated simple ideas to try and unite Germans against others and make them view the Nazis as the party that could make Germany great again. A key tactic was to encourage Germans to hate those countries which had signed the Treaty of Versailles by claiming that they had stolen German territory and treated Germany unfairly after the war.
- Nazi propaganda was very effective when it built on existing ideas. For example, the Nazis used lots of anti-communist and anti-Semitic themes in their propaganda. These prejudices already existed in Germany before the Nazis rose to power, so Nazi propaganda relating to Jewish people and communists appealed to many people.
- Nazi propaganda encouraged a return to traditional values and culture. Many people had disapproved of cultural changes during the Weimar Republic and thought the Weimar government was too liberal, so they were receptive to the Nazis' message that Germany should return to its traditional roots.

Life in Nazi Germany, 1933-39

Page 47 — Attitudes Towards the Church
Thinking Historically
1 a) Most Germans were Christians in the 1930s, so the Church had a lot of influence over people's beliefs and behaviour.
   b) The Church had played a big role in education in Weimar Germany. This gave the Church a lot of influence in young people's lives.
   c) Hitler was concerned that the Church might oppose him. Because the Church was so popular, opposition from the Church could have caused serious problems for the Nazis.
2 You can choose any of the factors, as long as you explain your answer. For example:
   The Church's popularity was the factor that made it seem the most threatening to the Nazis, because it meant that most people were likely to listen to the teachings of the Church as well as or instead of to the Nazis. If the Church wasn't so popular, then the Nazis wouldn't have been so concerned about the risk of opposition from the Church or the Church's role in education.

Knowledge and Understanding
1 The Concordat was an agreement between the Nazi Party and the Catholic Church — the Nazis promised to leave the Catholic Church alone as long as the Church promised not to interfere in politics.
2 Hitler and the Catholic Church had different reasons for signing the Concordat. Hitler wanted to restrict the power of the Catholic Church and make sure the Church wouldn't oppose him. The Catholic Church wanted to avoid confrontation with the Nazis and guarantee its survival in Nazi Germany.
3 Catholic Church:
   - The Concordat of July 1933 banned the Catholic Church from speaking out against the Nazis.
   - The Nazis gradually restricted Catholic influence in education, so that Catholic education was virtually destroyed by 1939.
   - Priests were arrested from 1935 and put on trial.
   - Catholic newspapers were suppressed.
   - Catholic youth groups were disbanded.

Protestant Church:
   - All the Protestant Churches were merged into the Reich Church in 1936.
   - The symbol of the cross was replaced with the Swastika and the Bible was replaced with 'Mein Kampf'.
   - Non-Aryan ministers were suspended and only Nazis could give sermons.
4 Here are some points your answer may include:
   - The Nazis' policies towards the Church helped to increase their control over German society because the Nazis were able to prevent the Church from opposing them directly, while slowly weakening the influence of the Church over the German people.
   - When the Nazis came to power in 1933, the Catholic and Protestant Churches had a big influence over education, politics and home life. By signing the Concordat, the Nazis were able to keep the Catholic Church away from politics, and they used their increasing political power to take control of education.
   - The Nazis weakened the influence of the Protestant Churches by combining them all under the banner of the Reich Church and replacing religious symbols with Nazi ones. By 'Nazifying' the Protestant Church, the Nazis ensured that only their views were spread during sermons.

Page 49 — Opposition
Knowledge and Understanding
1 a) • Members of the Communist Party (KPD) and Social Democratic Party (SPD).
   - Founded secret groups and organised strikes.
   - Had limited impact, as the Gestapo often found out about their plans and different parties didn't work together. The Nazis executed some party members.
   b) • Protestant pastor Martin Niemöller — one of the Confessing Church founders. Spoke out against the Nazis in a sermon and was then sent to a concentration camp.
   - Dietrich Bonhoeffer — a member of the Confessing Church. Helped Jews escape Germany and planned to assassinate Hitler. He was caught and executed by the Nazi Party.
   - Clemens August von Galen — Catholic bishop who used sermons to criticise Nazi racial policy and murder. The Nazis didn't execute him as they needed to ensure that German Catholics supported the party.
   c) • Opposed Nazi beliefs and the Hitler Youth.
   - Helped army deserters and those who were persecuted by the Nazis. They also distributed anti-Nazi leaflets.
   - As their resistance to the Nazis intensified, many members were arrested and some were even executed.
   d) • Opposed Nazi control over culture.
   - Listened to American music and drank alcohol.
   - The Nazis arrested some Swing Kids and some were sent to concentration camps.

Interpretation
1 Joll suggests that most people accepted the Nazi regime. He says that 'a majority of the German people had gone along with what Hitler did'. He argues that as a result of this, acts of opposition were rare, small-scale and secret — 'open opposition [was] almost impossible' and most protests 'remained personal'.

Answers

2 Here are some points your answer may include:
- Point — As Joll argues, 'Any open opposition' was very hard because the Nazis dealt with opposition so ruthlessly.
- Evidence — The police state was very effective at identifying and punishing opponents of the regime. Critics of the regime from both the Church and anti-Nazi youth groups were imprisoned or even executed.
- Why evidence supports point — Any attempt to oppose the Nazis, from serious political opposition to teenage rebellion, was extremely dangerous. This may well have made open opposition feel 'almost impossible' for most Germans.
- Point — As Joll argues, many 'German people had gone along with Hitler' — a lot of people supported at least some of the Nazis' policies.
- Evidence — The Nazis performed well in elections in the late 1920s and early 1930s. Many Germans shared some of Hitler's aims and beliefs, such as hatred of the Treaty of Versailles, anti-Semitism and a desire to return to traditional values.
- Why evidence supports point — This apparent support for the Nazis would have made it difficult for people to oppose them, because opponents would have felt they were not just fighting the Nazi regime, but the majority of the population.
- Point — Some people opposed the Nazis publicly.
- Evidence — Martin Niemöller opposed the Nazis publicly by setting up the Confessing Church and preaching anti-Nazi messages in a public sermon. Clemens August von Galen also used his sermons to protest against the Nazis. The Edelweiss Pirates made their protests public when they began distributing anti-Nazi leaflets.
- Why evidence supports point — These examples of public protest suggest that open opposition to the Nazis wasn't quite as difficult as Joll suggests. It was, however, very dangerous — many of those who publicly opposed the Nazis were harshly punished.

Page 51 — Work and Home
Thinking Historically
1 a) • Positive effects — Women who wanted to marry and have a family were supported by the Nazis. Awards were given to women who had large families and financial aid was offered to married couples.
- Negative effects — Women had less freedom. They were expected to stay at home and have children. They were prevented from doing certain jobs and encouraged to dress plainly and avoid make-up and smoking.
b) • Positive effects — Unemployment fell dramatically after 1933 due to the Nazis' public works programmes, conscription and rearmament. The National Labour Service gave jobs to men aged 18 to 25.
- Negative effects — Conscription and the National Labour Service meant that unemployed people could be forced to take on jobs against their will. The Nazis only guaranteed jobs for 'Aryan' men — not women or Jews.

c) • Positive effects — Workers could aspire to own a Volkswagen. The 'Strength through Joy' scheme provided workers with cheap holidays and leisure activities. Factory owners were encouraged to improve conditions for workers through the 'Beauty of Labour' scheme.
- Negative effects — Trade Unions were banned and workers were forced to join the Nazis' Labour Front. Workers weren't allowed to strike or resign. Wages remained low even though the cost of living rose by about 25%.
d) • Positive effects — Small-business owners were able to advance more in society than they'd been able to before. Many in the middle classes felt better off.
- Negative effects — Small businesses had to pay higher taxes.
2 Some Germans felt that their quality of life improved because the Nazis made positive changes to living and working conditions, especially for 'Aryan' men. After the years of the Great Depression, when unemployment reached one third of all workers, the years of the Nazi regime seemed much better to many, because unemployment was virtually wiped out. The Nazis also made efforts to make workers and 'Aryans' feel supported by the state and included in the Volksgemeinschaft. Women who wanted large families were compensated financially, while workers were supported by a range of schemes, such as the 'Strength through Joy' and 'Beauty of Labour' schemes.

Source Analysis
1 a) • The ideal German family was 'Aryan' — all of the people in the poster are blond and have light skin.
- The ideal German family was made up of a husband, a wife and several children. The poster shows a couple with three children of different ages.
b) • The Nazi Party intended to play a central role in German society. The text explains that 'the Nazi Party secures the Volksgemeinschaft', which suggests that the Nazi Party holds the community together.
- The Nazi Party would protect people. The eagle in the poster represents the Nazi Party and is shown protecting the family with its wings.
c) • The Volksgemeinschaft was intended to operate on both a national and a local level. The text explains that the Volksgemeinschaft is a 'national community' but it is supported by 'local' groups.
- The Nazi Party presented itself as a central part of the Volksgemeinschaft. The text claims that 'the Nazi Party secures the Volksgemeinschaft'.
2 The source is a propaganda poster, so its purpose was to convince people to follow the Nazis' model of family life. For this reason, it is useful in showing the role that the Nazis expected women to follow in the 1930s. However, the usefulness of the source is limited for an investigation into the role women actually played because it doesn't provide any evidence for the extent to which women followed the role promoted by the Nazis.

Page 53 — Young People
Source Analysis
1 a) The Nazis portrayed the Hitler Youth as a military-style organisation that encouraged discipline and prepared young men for war.

Answers

b) The Nazis portrayed members of the Hitler Youth as very powerful and influential compared to ordinary people.

c) The Nazis made the Hitler Youth seem important by suggesting that they had a role in protecting society from 'troublemakers'.

d) The Nazis emphasised that joining the Hitler Youth would make boys strong and powerful. They were taking on a serious role as defenders of the German people.

e) The Nazis presented the Hitler Youth as a united organisation. It offered boys a sense of belonging and identity.

2   The poster might have encouraged some young people to join the Hitler Youth because it suggests that the Hitler Youth was an exciting and important organisation to be involved in. The poster stresses that young people are brought together by the Hitler Youth and suggests that they can become strong and powerful by joining up.

3   I think the source would be most useful for investigation c), because the purpose of the poster is to promote the Hitler Youth. Therefore, the source can help us to understand what young people might have expected to get out of the Hitler Youth and why they might have found it appealing.

4   • The source would be less useful for investigation a) because it only shows us how the Nazis chose to present the Hitler Youth and not what life was actually like for Hitler Youth members.

   • The source would be less useful for investigation b) because it was made in 1936, so it isn't that relevant to the popularity of the Hitler Youth in the 1920s. The source can't tell us if the poster persuaded young people to join the Hitler Youth, so it doesn't provide any information about how popular the Hitler Youth was.

Thinking Historically

1   • Teachers were made to join the Nazi Teachers' Association and trained in Nazi methods. — The Nazi Party wanted to ensure that teachers were following their programmes and knew what message to give to children.

   • Children were encouraged to report teachers who didn't use proper Nazi methods. — The Nazis wanted to ensure that all teachers were loyal Nazis and were spreading their message.

   • Subjects were rewritten to fit with Nazi ideas, such as anti-Semitism and hatred of communism. — The Nazi Party wanted to raise a generation of loyal Nazis who shared their core beliefs.

   • Physical education became more important. — The Nazis wanted to prepare boys for joining the army.

   • Anti-Nazi and Jewish books were burned in universities. — The Nazis wanted to censor any views that opposed their own.

   • Jewish lecturers and teachers were sacked. — The Nazis wanted to exclude Jewish people from public life and prevent them from influencing young people.

Page 55 — Nazi Discrimination

Knowledge and Understanding

1   • 1933 — The SA organises a boycott of Jewish businesses across Germany. The boycott leads to a lot of violence against Jews. It is unpopular with the German people.

   • 1935 — The Nuremberg Laws are passed. Jews lose many legal rights and are made to seem inferior to 'Aryan' Germans. Jews are no longer considered German citizens. They cannot marry non-Jews or have sexual relationships with them.

   • 1938 — By this point, Jewish children can no longer go to school and many Jews are prevented from going to public places like theatres.

   • November 1938 — After the murder of a German diplomat in Paris by a Jew, the Nazis organise a series of anti-Jewish riots (known as Kristallnacht). Many Jewish shops are destroyed and synagogues across Germany are burnt down. Thousands of Jews are arrested and sent to concentration camps.

Source Analysis

1 a) The source is useful because its author lived in Nazi Germany and used to shop in Jewish stores, so she witnessed how the Nazis managed to make Jewish people increasingly isolated over time. However, the usefulness of the source is limited because the author is not Jewish, so she cannot give a first-hand account of how the Nazis' anti-Semitic policies affected Jewish people themselves.

   b) The source comes from an interview many years after the fall of the Nazis. This makes it useful because it means that Helga Schmidt would have been able to speak freely about the impact of the Nazis' anti-Semitic policies.

   c) The content of the source is useful because it shows how the Nazis' anti-Semitic policies affected the behaviour of non-Jewish Germans. It also provides evidence that the Nazis' policies made Jewish people increasingly isolated by making non-Jewish people afraid to interact with them. However, the source doesn't directly tell us how Jewish people's lives were affected by the Nazis' policies.

Interpretation

1   Kaplan's main argument is that Jewish people became increasingly isolated because Germans who had previously supported them did not speak out against the Nazis' anti-Semitic persecution. Kaplan describes these people 'remaining silent rather than defending Jews' after 1933.

2   In her interview, Helga Schmidt explains that many Germans like her 'didn't trust ourselves anymore' to shop in Jewish stores. This supports Kaplan's argument that 'customers who were loyal at first began to dwindle as the government increased its attack on Jewish businesses.'

Pages 60-62 — Exam-Style Questions

1 This question is level marked. How to grade your answer:

Level 1 1-2 marks	The answer gives a simple analysis of the sources to come to a basic judgement about their usefulness. It shows a basic understanding of the sources' content and/or provenance, as well as displaying some relevant knowledge of the topic.
Level 2 3-5 marks	The answer analyses the sources in more detail to make judgements about their usefulness. It shows a good understanding of the sources' content and/or provenance and uses relevant knowledge to support its judgements.
Level 3 6-8 marks	The answer evaluates the sources to make judgements about their usefulness. It shows a detailed understanding of the sources and uses relevant knowledge to analyse their content and provenance, and to support its judgements.

Here are some points your answer may include:
*   Source A is useful because it was written by someone who actually was a young person in Nazi Germany. Therefore, it provides a first-hand view of how successfully the Nazis controlled young people.
*   Source A is useful because it directly shows how education was used to control young people, how it was received and how effective it was in shaping their attitudes.
*   Source A is useful because it was written a long time after the fall of the Nazis, so the author would not have been afraid to speak openly. However, the author might have mis-remembered exactly how he felt as a child and what life in Nazi Germany was really like. This limits the usefulness of the source.
*   The usefulness of Source A is limited because it represents the view of an individual who was a young child when the Nazis came to power. Others might have had very different experiences — Source B, for example, suggests that not all young people accepted Nazi control in the same way as Heck.
*   Source B is useful because it is an anti-Nazi song that was sung by members of a youth group that opposed the Nazis, so it demonstrates that the Nazis didn't manage to control all young people successfully.
*   Source B is useful because it shows that, far from being controlled by the Nazis, some young people hoped to 'break the chains' of the Nazi regime and fight for 'young people's freedom'. However, the usefulness of the source is limited, because it doesn't show whether the people who sang this song ever took any other action against the Nazis.

2 This question is level marked. How to grade your answer:

Level 1 1-2 marks	The answer gives a difference, but it is only loosely supported by reference to the interpretations.
Level 2 3-4 marks	The answer give a key difference, which is well supported by reference to both interpretations.

Here are some points your answer may include:
*   Interpretation 1 argues that the Nazis successfully controlled young people by teaching them to share Nazi 'attitudes and beliefs'. The author claims that more young people became anti-Semitic due to the effectiveness of Nazi propaganda and teaching. Interpretation 2, on the other hand, states that the Nazis weren't very successful at controlling young people. It argues that many young people 'rejected the values taught' by the Nazi Party and chose to form opposition groups, such as the Edelweiss Pirates.
*   Interpretation 1 argues that young people were successfully controlled, as they were passive victims of Nazi education and propaganda. They were 'strongly malleable' and couldn't avoid Nazi influence. However, Interpretation 2 argues that many young people actively challenged the ideas they were being taught and opposed Nazi control, even when their lives were in danger.

3 This question is level marked. How to grade your answer:

Level 1 1-2 marks	The answer gives a basic explanation of reasons why the interpretations are different. This is based on a simple analysis of the interpretations or on knowledge of the topic.
Level 2 3-4 marks	The answer gives a detailed explanation of reasons why the interpretations are different. This is well supported by a detailed analysis of the interpretations and knowledge of the topic.

Here are some points your answer may include:
*   The authors might express different views because the interpretations are focusing on young people of different ages. Interpretation 1 focuses on schoolchildren, who were taught to believe Nazi ideas from a young age. Interpretation 2 focuses particularly on adolescents who formed opposition groups such as the Edelweiss Pirates.
*   The authors might express different views because they are based on different sources. For example, Interpretation 1 is supported by Source A, which states that Nazi education techniques successfully controlled young people, whereas Interpretation 2 is supported by Source B, which is an example of how opposition groups resisted the Nazis and their control.
*   The authors might express different views because the interpretations are partial extracts. Interpretation 1 focuses on how Nazi education techniques and propaganda successfully controlled young people, without mentioning opposition groups. Interpretation 2, however, focuses only on opposition groups. It doesn't address the use of education and propaganda to control young people.

Answers

4 This question is level marked. How to grade your answer:

Level 1 1-4 marks	The answer either supports or disagrees with the interpretation. This is based on a simple analysis of one interpretation and basic knowledge of the topic.
Level 2 5-8 marks	The answer shows support or disagreement by evaluating the interpretation. The evaluation draws on analysis of both interpretations and some relevant knowledge of the topic. An overall judgement is made, but it isn't well supported by the answer.
Level 3 9-12 marks	The answer shows support or disagreement by evaluating the interpretation in detail. The evaluation draws on a detailed analysis of both interpretations, which considers their different viewpoints and shows a good level of relevant knowledge. An overall judgement is made that is partly supported by the answer.
Level 4 13-16 marks	The answer considers both sides of the argument. It draws on an accurate and detailed analysis of both interpretations, which considers their different viewpoints and shows an excellent level of relevant knowledge. An overall judgement is made that is well supported by the answer.

Here are some points your answer may include:

- Interpretation 1 argues that the Nazis used education to successfully control young people's 'attitudes and beliefs'. This argument is convincing because the Nazis changed all aspects of the education system in order to control young people. For example, most teachers were members of the Nazi Teachers' Association and subjects were rewritten to teach Nazi ideas and shape young people's views. This meant that everything young people were exposed to throughout their education was based on Nazi ideology, which would have made it very difficult for young people to avoid being influenced by Nazi ideas.
- Interpretation 1 claims that the Nazis were 'ambitious in their attempt to indoctrinate the population'. This is supported by the fact that their efforts to influence young people went far beyond education. Youth organisations like the Hitler Youth and League of German Maidens ensured that young people were also taught Nazi ideas outside of school. After 1936, the Hitler Youth became all but compulsory, meaning that young people's lives were almost entirely structured by the Nazis. This demonstrates how the Nazis successfully controlled young people by influencing most aspects of their lives.
- Interpretation 1 suggests that 'propaganda and schooling were highly effective in changing attitudes and beliefs'. The effectiveness of these techniques can be seen in how fanatically some Hitler Youth members fought when they were eventually called up to help the war effort. The fact that many young people grew up to share Nazi beliefs and serve the party suggests that the Nazis successfully controlled young people.

- Interpretation 1 implies that very few young people opposed the Nazis. Although some young people joined opposition groups such as the Edelweiss Pirates, they were not typical of young people in Germany. Membership of these groups was quite limited, and so Interpretation 1 is convincing when it claims that the Nazis successfully controlled most young people.
- Despite this, the significance of the opposition youth groups should not be overlooked. Interpretation 2 argues that 'many teenagers rejected the values taught in the Hitler Youth'. Some of these young people went on to form groups like the Edelweiss Pirates and the Swing Kids, who resisted the Nazis by distributing anti-Nazi leaflets, helping army deserters and forced labourers, or simply by listening to American music and drinking alcohol. This suggests that in some cases the Nazis' attempts to control young people actually encouraged them to rebel.
- Interpretation 2 suggests that in the late 1930s 'some young people began to question the Nazi regime'. Towards the end of the 1930s, attendance at the Hitler Youth fell when it took on a more military focus. This suggests that there were some limits to the Nazis' control over young people — by the late 1930s, some young people did not share the Nazis' desire for war and were attempting to escape the influence of Nazi youth groups.

5 Each inference is marked separately. You can have up to two marks per inference. How to grade your answer:
- 1 mark for giving one credible inference.
- 2 marks for giving one credible inference and using content from the source to back it up.

Here are some points your answer may include:
- The Nazi persecution of the Jews was very public. The men in the photograph are being made to walk publicly through the streets, as people watch in the background.
- The Nazis' anti-Semitic persecution aimed to humiliate Jewish people. In the photo, the Nazis have attempted to humiliate a group of Jewish men by publicly parading them down the street, marking them out as different with a large Star of David and demonstrating how powerless they are in the face of the Nazi regime.
- The persecution of Jewish people in Nazi Germany was official and organised. The presence of Nazi officers in uniform and the organised nature of the parade suggests that this kind of persecution was officially authorised by the Nazi Party.

6 This question is level marked. How to grade your answer:

Level 1 1-3 marks	Limited knowledge and understanding of the period is shown. The answer gives a simple explanation of why the Nazi Party tried to control the Church. Ideas are generally unconnected and don't follow a logical order.
Level 2 4-6 marks	Some relevant knowledge and understanding of the period is shown. The answer gives a basic analysis of some of the reasons why the Nazi Party tried to control the Church. An attempt has been made to organise ideas in a logical way.

Level 3 7-9 marks	A good level of knowledge and understanding of the period is shown. The answer explores multiple reasons why the Nazi Party tried to control the Church. It identifies some relevant connections between different points, and ideas are organised logically.
Level 4 10-12 marks	**Answers can't be awarded Level 4 if they only discuss the information suggested in the question.** Knowledge and understanding of the period is precise and detailed. The answer considers a range of reasons why the Nazi Party tried to control the Church and analyses each one. All ideas are organised logically and connections between different points are identified to create a developed analysis of the topic.

Here are some points your answer may include:

- In the 1930s, most Germans were Christians, so the Church was very influential. The Nazis wanted to control the Church because it influenced how people lived their lives and, if left unchecked, could challenge the Nazis' messages and policies.

- The Nazis tried to control the Church because it had traditionally played an important role in German politics. During the Weimar Republic, the Church had worked with the state on significant matters, such as education. The Nazi Party wanted complete control over politics and education, so it tried to bring the Church under its control.

- The Nazi Party tried to control the Church because they saw an opportunity to use the Church's influence in order to spread Nazi ideology. In 1936, Hitler merged Germany's Protestant Churches into the Reich Church, in which the cross was replaced by the swastika, and the Bible by 'Mein Kampf'. Although the Reich Church claimed to be a religious organisation, its main goal was to spread the Nazi Party's messages.

- The Nazis tried to control the Church because there was a risk Church leaders would use their sermons to criticise the Nazis. For example, the Catholic bishop Clemens August von Galen used his sermons to protest against Nazi ideas. The Nazis felt unable to execute von Galen because they feared this would turn German Catholics against them. This shows why it was so important to the Nazis to control the messages spread by the Church.

- The Nazi Party tried to control the Church because the Church had the potential to form an organised opposition movement. For example, Martin Niemöller founded the Confessing Church as a protest against the Nazis' creation of the Reich Church. The power and influence of the Church meant that any organised resistance like this could be very dangerous to Hitler's regime.

Index